Cityrack
Berlin

**CHRISTOPHER AND
MELANIE RICE**

Christopher Rice writes regularly on Eastern Europe and Russia and holds a PhD from the Centre for Russian and East European Studies at Birmingham University. His wife, Melanie, is also a writer and shares his fascination with this part of the world. The Rices have written a number of guidebooks including Berlin *in the AA/Thomas Cook series.*

GW01464085

For city-centre map see inside back cover

AA Publishing

Contents

life **5 – 12**

Introducing Berlin	6–7	A Chronology	10–11
Berlin in Figures	8	People & Events	
Berlin People	9	from History	12

how to organise your time **13 – 22**

Itineraries	14–15	Organised Sightseeing	19
Walks	16–17	Excursions	20–23
Evening Strolls	18	What's On	24

top 25 sights **23 – 48**

1 Sanssouci	24	**16** Brandenburg Gate	39
2 Cecilienhof	25	**17** Checkpoint Charlie	40
3 Klein-Glienicke	26	**18** Gendarmenmarkt	41
4 Spandau	27	**19** Unter den Linden	42
5 Grunewald	28	**20** Museums Island	
6 Sachsenhausen		(Museumsinsel)	43
Concentration Camp	29	**21** Pergamon Museum	44
7 Ethnographical		**22** Berlin Cathedral	
Museum (Museum für		(Berliner Dom)	45
Völkerkunde)	30	**23** Nikolaiviertel	46
8 Schloss		**24** Alexanderplatz	47
Charlottenburg	31	**25** Schloss Köpenick	48
9 Kurfürstendamm	32		
10 Kaiser Wilhelm			
Memorial Church			
(Gedächtniskirche)	33		
11 Bauhaus Museum	34		
12 Kulturforum	35		
13 Museum of Applied Art	36		
14 Tiergarten	37		
15 Topography of Terror	38		

Index...94–95 •

About this book...4

best 49 – 60

MUSEUMS	50–51	VIEWS	57
GALLERIES	52	STATUES & MONUMENTS	58
PLACES OF WORSHIP	53	ATTRACTIONS FOR	
BRIDGES	54	CHILDREN	59
POLITICAL SIGHTS	55	FREE ATTRACTIONS	60
PARKS & GARDENS	56		

where to... 61 – 86

EAT	62–69	ANTIQUES, GLASS &	
GERMAN RESTAURANTS	62–63	PORCELAIN	74
INTERNATIONAL		MARKETS & FOODSHOPS	75
RESTAURANTS	64–65	THE BEST OF THE REST	76–77
ASIAN & VEGETARIAN			
RESTAURANTS	66	**BE ENTERTAINED**	78–83
MIDDLE EASTERN, TURKISH		THEATRES & CONCERTS	78
& OUT-OF-TOWN		CABARET	79
RESTAURANTS	67	PUBS, BARS & CLUBS	80–81
CAFÉS	68–69	FOLK, JAZZ & ROCK	82
		SPORTS	83
SHOP	70–77		
DEPARTMENT STORES &		**STAY**	84–86
SOUVENIRS	70	LUXURY HOTELS	84
BOUTIQUES & DESIGNER		MID-RANGE HOTELS	85
CLOTHES	71	BUDGET ACCOMMODATION	86
SECONDHAND & OFFBEAT	72		
GALLERIES	73		

travel facts 87 – 93

ARRIVING & DEPARTING	88	MEDIA & COMMUNICATIONS	91–92
ESSENTIAL FACTS	88–90	EMERGENCIES	92–93
PUBLIC TRANSPORT	90–91	LANGUAGE	93

CREDITS, ACKNOWLEDGEMENTS AND TITLES IN THIS SERIES 96

About this book

ORGANISATION

Citypack Berlin's six sections cover the six most important aspects of your visit to Berlin:

- Berlin life – the city and its people
- Itineraries, walks, and excursions – how to organise your time
- The top 25 sights, numbered 1–25 from west to east across the city
- Features about different aspects of the city that make it special
- Detailed listings of restaurants, hotels, shops and nightlife
- Practical information

In addition, text boxes provide fascinating extra facts and snippets, highlights of places to visit, and invaluable practical advice.

CROSS-REFERENCES

To help you make the most of your visit, cross-references, indicated by ➤ , show you where to find additional information about a place or subject.

MAPS

- **The fold-out map** in the wallet at the back of the book is a comprehensive street plan of Berlin. All the map references given in the book refer to this map. For example, the Museum of Applied Art, on Tiergartenstrasse, has the following information: ✚ C6 – indicating the grid square of the map in which the Museum of Applied Art will be found.
- **The city-centre maps** found on the inside front and back covers of the book itself are for quick reference. They show the Top 25 Sights, described on pages 24–48, which are clearly plotted by number (**1** – **25**, not page number) from west to east.

PRICES

Where appropriate, an indication of the cost of an establishment is given by **£** signs: **£££** denotes higher prices, **££** denotes average prices, while **£** denotes lower charges.

BERLIN
life

Introducing Berlin   *6–7*

Berlin in Figures   *8*

Berlin People   *9*

A Chronology   *10–11*

*People & Events
   from History*   *12*

INTRODUCING BERLIN

Potsdamer Platz

Europe's largest building site, covering an area of 68,000sq m, is currently being developed around this historic square. Its chief sponsors, Daimler-Benz and Sony, have commissioned some of Europe's most innovative architects, including Renzo Piano and Richard Rogers, to create an ambitious new business and entertainment focus for the city. More than 7,500 Berliners will live and work here when the development is completed.

Chinese Teahouse in the park at Sanssouci

NEW LOOK

Berliners, more than most, will be looking forward to the dawn of the new millennium, when the city will formally become the capital of a unified Germany. To say that Berlin is undergoing a face-lift in readiness is an under-statement. The entire city centre has been transformed into one gigantic construction site, an irritant to motorists and commuters, no doubt, but it will be a blessing for the citizens in the long run.

By the first decade of the new century there will be a newly refurbished Reichstag building on the edge of the Tiergarten; a sprawling amalgam of offices, apartments, hotels and shopping and leisure facilities on the site of what was once Potsdamer Platz; a metro line intended to link up the dispersed commercial centres of East and West; housing developments on the city's periphery and, rumour has it, a new international airport.

Berlin has always lacked a fixed identity; it is constantly in a state of flux, 'always becoming, never being'. The city shrugs off the many varied layers of its past like so many discarded clothes: the baroque grandeur of the Gendarmenmarkt, the rococo provincialism of the Nikolaiviertel, the Prussian pomp of Unter den Linden and Museums Island, the twin polarities of the Ku'damm and Alexanderplatz, remnants of an ideological rivalry finally consigned to history. Now, restless as ever, Berlin is casting about for a new set of architectural clothes in time for the millennium.

COUNTRY IN THE CITY

At the last count there were over 2,000 building sites in Berlin, so it is just as well that as much as one-third of the city is green space. Berliners use this embarrassment of riches to full advan-tage. Every weekend you will find them setting out from the boating marinas at Wannsee for the placid waters of the Havel. Ornithologists go bird-watching on the shores of the Müggelsee, dog-owners head for the Grunewald forest, hikers for the woodland around the Schorfheide. There are even beaches in this land-locked city. Nor is it necessary to travel far, as Berlin's army of office workers will tell you. The city's most famous park, the Tiergarten – an oasis of rural tranquillity – is only a stone's throw from the mayhem of Zoo station at the heart of the city.

Sculpture in the Breitscheidplatz

BERLINERS

Berliners are a restless and energetic people. Their chief characteristic, remarked on by other Germans as *Berliner Schnauze* ('Berlin mouth'), implies both a taste for quick-fire humour and repartee and a tendency to show off and boast. Most visitors will find the people genial and easy-going: they wear their much-heralded industriousness lightly. There is still some friction between 'Ossis' and 'Wessis' as the former try to adjust to the values of Western yuppiedom, while the latter sometimes resent the competition for jobs and services and the fact that, for some time to come, they will be expected to subsidise their fellow citizens.

Berlin's cosmopolitan feel (typified by the internationalism of the restaurants to be found around Savignyplatz, for example), is somewhat misleading. Actually the city is under-represented where immigrants are concerned, with one notable exception. The old working-class suburb of Kreuzberg is sometimes called 'little Istanbul': its large Turkish population adds a colourful, exotic ingredient to the Berlin persona.

Seat of government

A new parliamentary quarter is being developed in the Tiergarten between the revamped Reichstag building and the 18th-century Schloss Bellevue (official seat of the Federal President). The ministries will be located in the old Regierungsviertel (government quarter), to the south of Unter den Linden. The move from Bonn to Berlin is expected to entail the creation of 12,000 Federal jobs in the new capital.

BERLIN IN FIGURES

POPULATION AND GROWTH

- The population of Berlin (1998) is 3,470,000
- 46 per cent are male; 54 per cent are female; the only Berlin district with more men than women is Kreuzberg
- 12 per cent of the population are foreign, of which more than one-third are Turkish
- 27 per cent are under 25 years of age; 14 per cent are over 65
- Historical growth:
  1600 – 9,000 inhabitants
  1709 – 57,000
  1800 – 172,000
  1900 – 1,888,000
  1920 – 3,879,000
- The municipal reform of 1920 made Greater Berlin the largest city on the European continent.

ENVIRONMENT

- Berlin's municipal area is 889sq km, an area 9 times greater than that of Paris
- 24 per cent of Greater Berlin consists of rivers, lakes and forests; 10.9 per cent is recreational
- The highest natural hill is Grosse Müggelberg (only 115m)
- Germany's northernmost vineyard is on Berlin's Kreuzberg
- Berlin has 1,800,000 dwellings; 953 bridges; 5,113km of public streets; 197km of navigable waterways
- Berlin has one of the most extensive public transport networks in Europe with 9 U-Bahn lines; 12 S-Bahn lines; 26 tram lines; 155 day bus lines; 445 night bus lines; more than 1 billion passengers use the system annually

LEISURE

- Each year there are more than 32,000,000 visits to Berlin's theatres, cinemas and palaces
- Berlin has 3 opera houses; 150 theatres and concert halls; 200 fringe theatres; 50 children's theatres; 170 museums; 9 palaces; 274 libraries; 1,900 sports clubs; 7,000 cafés, restaurants and pubs

BERLIN PEOPLE

EBERHARD DIEPGEN

Born in Berlin in November 1941, Berlin's mayor, Eberhard Diepgen, was educated at the Free University of (West) Berlin. He joined the Christian Democrat Party while still a student and went on to chair the West Berlin party organisation. A member of the Berlin Chamber of Deputies from 1971 to 1981, he was also a deputy in the German Bundestag (Parliament). He was elected Mayor of Berlin in 1984 and was in the happy position of presiding over the unification celebrations in 1990. Diepgen is excited by the prospect of the arrival of the Federal German parliament and government at the end of 1999. In a recent speech he described Berlin as a 'city in transition', assigning it a future role as 'the workshop of German unity…setting an example for the rest of the country in bringing Easterners and Westerners together'.

Dietrich Fischer-Dieskau

Renowned German baritone Dietrich Fischer-Dieskau was born in Berlin in 1925 and began his singing career at the Berlin State Opera. Since then he has won numerous musical awards, especially for his recordings (more than one Grammy for example). Best known throughout his career for his interpretation of German Lieder, he has also premiered works by Britten, Henze and others. He lives in Charlottenburg.

Claudio Abbado

CLAUDIO ABBADO

When the Italian conductor Claudio Abbado succeeded the legendary Herbert von Karajan as Artistic Director of the Berlin Philharmonic Orchestra in October 1989, he had already, at the age of 55, established himself as one of the world's leading interpreters of the classical repertoire with organisations as prestigious as La Scala Milan, the London Symphony Orchestra and the Vienna Opera. In stark contrast to the autocratic von Karajan, Abbado has encouraged a team spirit with the Berlin musicians that has endeared him to them and has led to the remarkable decision, by unanimous vote of the members, to extend his contract to the year 2002. Abbadio has introduced new initiatives, including collaborative ventures with Berlin theatres.

A Chronology

1244	First recorded mention of Berlin
1369	Berlin becomes a member of the trading association known as the Hanseatic League
1443	Frederick II of Brandenburg builds the first Berlin castle (Schloss)
1448	Berliners defend their privileges in the revolt known as 'Berliner Unwille'
1618–48	Berlin is devastated by Austrian and Swedish armies during the Thirty Years' War and the population is halved to under 6,000
1701	Elector Frederick III proclaims himself King Frederick I of Prussia
1740	Accession of Frederick the Great
1806	Napoleon enters Berlin
1847	Werner Siemens and Johann Georg Halske manufacture the first telegraph in a house on Schöneberger Strasse
1848	Germany's 'bourgeois revolution'; demands for greater middle-class representation in government; workers take to the barricades
1871	Berlin becomes the capital of a united German Empire under Kaiser Wilhelm I and the Prime Minister of Prussia, Prince Otto von Bismarck
1881	The world's first electric streetcar goes into service in Berlin
1918	After World War I, Kaiser Wilhelm II abdicates to make way for a German Republic
1920s	Against a background of growing social and economic instability, Berlin becomes a cultural powerhouse and entertainment centre. Einstein, Brecht, Gropius and Grosz all flourish
1933	Adolf Hitler becomes Chancellor of Germany

1936	Berlin plays host to the Olympic Games. Black American athlete Jesse Owens triumphs on the field, film-maker Leni Riefenstahl celebrates the games in *Olympia*
1938	On Reichskristallnacht (the 'night of breaking glass') the Nazis orchestrate the destruction of Jewish property and synagogues
1939–45	World War II
1945	Berlin lies in ruins; the population is reduced from 4 million to 2.8 million. The city is divided into four zones of occupation, administered by French, British, US and Soviet forces
1948–9	An attempt by the Soviet government to force the Western Allies to withdraw from Berlin by blockading the city is foiled by a gigantic airlift of food, medicines, clothing and supplies
1949	Germany is divided into the Federal Republic and the German Democratic Republic, leaving Berlin stranded in the communist GDR
1953	Construction workers in East Berlin, protesting about low wages, provoke a full-scale uprising which is put down by Soviet tanks
1961	The flood of East Berliners to the West is staunched by the building of the Berlin Wall
1963	John F Kennedy demonstrates American support for West Berlin in his famous 'Ich bin ein Berliner' speech at Schöneberg Town Hall
1989	On 9 November the collapse of communism in Eastern Europe leads to the opening of the Wall and its eventual demise
1994	The last of the occupying Allied and Soviet forces formally withdraw from Berlin
2000	Berlin once again becomes the capital of Germany

PEOPLE & EVENTS FROM HISTORY

Imperial disdain

Surprisingly, Kaiser Wilhelm II was less enthusiastic about Berlin than many of his imperial predecessors. In 1892 he rejected his Chancellor's proposal for a world fair in the city, commenting:

'There is nothing in Berlin that can captivate the foreigner, except a few museums, castles and soldiers. After six days, the red book in hand, he has seen everything and departs relieved, feeling that he has done his duty.'

FREDERICK THE GREAT

The great Prussian monarch was a living contradiction, who had a profound impact on the future of Berlin and of Germany. An enthusiast of the Enlightenment with its emphasis on rationalism, tolerance and intellectual curiosity (Voltaire was a guest at the Prussian court), his first action on the European political stage was aggressive – the cynical exploitation of Austrian weakness by the invasion of Silesia.

NAPOLEON

When Napoleon ordered the occupation of Berlin in 1806 he did not realise that he was sowing the seeds of his own destruction. His actions served as a powerful stimulus to Prussian patriotism, galvanising politicians into making the military and institutional reforms that led to the historic defeat of the French at Leipzig in 1813. In strengthening the Prussian nation at the expense of Austria, Napoleon also unwittingly contributed to German unification.

ADOLF HITLER

An Austrian by birth and a Bavarian in his sympathies, the German Führer regarded Berlin with undisguised distaste, partly because, as a hotbed of Communism and radical protest, it was the last bulwark of resistance to the Nazi regime. However, Berlin's place at the political heart of the regime singled it out for special attention from the Allies through the last months of World War II. By 1945 Hitler's boast that he would transform Berlin into a new world capital, Germania, had a hollow ring.

THE END OF THE WALL

For 40 years after the end of World War II, Berlin was an island of Western democratic values in a sea of Communist totalitarianism. The building of the Berlin Wall in 1961, a knee-jerk response to the growing exodus of Berliners from East to West, brought ideological confrontation into even sharper focus. The opening of the Wall in November 1989 was consequently a deeply symbolic moment in modern European history.

Statue of Frederick the Great, Unter den Linden

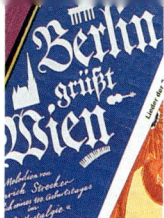

BERLIN
how to organise your time

ITINERARIES   *14–15*

The Ku'damm, Tiergarten &
   Unter den Linden
Schloss Charlottenburg &
   the Wannsee
Museuminsel, Alexanderplatz
   & the Nicolaiviertel
Sanssouci & Potsdam

WALKS   *16–17*

Prenzlauer Berg & the
   Scheunenviertel
Schöneberg

EVENING STROLLS   *18*

ORGANISED
  SIGHTSEEING   *19*

EXCURSIONS   *20–21*

Bernau
Lutherstadt Wittenberg

Lübbenau
Brandenburg

WHAT'S ON   *22*

ITINERARIES

Berlin is so large, and offers such a wealth of places to visit, that planning your sightseeing can be a daunting prospect. These four suggested one-day itineraries will help you cover some of the major sights in a practical way.

ITINERARY ONE	**THE KU'DAMM, TIERGARTEN & UNTER DEN LINDEN**
Morning	Stroll eastwards along the Ku'damm (► 32), from Adenauerplatz U-Bahn station for a morning of shopping and people-watching Pause for coffee in Café Kranzler (► 68) Later, visit the Kaiser Wilhelm Memorial Church (► 33) in Breitscheidplatz
Lunch	Shop in the food hall of KaDeWe (► 70) and have a picnic in the Tiergarten (► 37)
Afternoon	Take bus 100 from Zoo station or the Tiergarten to the Brandenburg Gate (► 39) Walk across Pariser Platz and along part of Unter den Linden, turning off to reach Französische Strasse U-Bahn station Take the U-Bahn southwards to Kochstrasse and visit the Haus am Checkpoint Charlie Museum (► 40)
ITINERARY TWO	**SCHLOSS CHARLOTTENBURG & THE WANNSEE**
Morning	Travel to Richard-Wagner-Platz U-Bahn station (or take bus 145 from Zoo station) and visit the former royal palace, Schloss Charlottenburg (► 31). Spend some time in the gardens, too. Cross Spandauer Damm to view the treasures of the Egyptian Museum (► 51) or the Berggruen Collection (► 52)
Lunch	Restaurant Eosander (► 69)
Afternoon	Take the S-Bahn (line 3) to Wannsee for an afternoon on the largest inland beach in Europe. or one of the many possible boat trips. Bus 116 will take you to the Glienicker Bridge (► 26), bus 216 to the ferry (daily 8–8) for Pfaueninsel (Peacock Island)(► 59)

ITINERARY THREE	**MUSEUMSINSEL, ALEXANDERPLATZ & THE NIKOLAIVIERTEL**
Morning	Take bus 100 or the U- or S-Bahn to Friedrichstrasse. Cross the footbridge from Am Kupfergraben to reach Museumsinsel (Museums Island), and spend the morning in the Pergamon Museum (► 44) The museum café is good for a coffee or snack.
Lunch	The terrace of the popular Opernpalais café and restaurant (► 69) near Museumsinsel
Afternoon	Walk west along Unter den Linden (► 42) and turn left at the statue of Frederick the Great into Bebelplatz. Cross Französische Strasse into Gendarmenmarkt (► 41) Walk to Stadtmitte U-Bahn station and travel to Alexanderplatz (► 47). Explore the scenic Nikolaiviertel (► 46) and its cafés
ITINERARY FOUR	**SANSSOUCI & POTSDAM**
Morning	Travel to Potsdam Stadt S-Bahn station and take bus A1 to Sanssouci (► 24). After visiting the Schloss, stroll through the grounds, perhaps lingering over a coffee at the Drachenhaus
Lunch	Choose one of Potsdam's many cafés, perhaps the café in the Film Museum (► 51)
Afternoon	Wander through Potsdam's charming old streets, such as Brandenburger Strasse, Dortustrasse, Am Neuer Markt and Lindenstrasse. The Dutch Quarter (Holländisches Viertel), with its neat rows of redbrick, gabled houses, was built in the 18th century for construction workers labouring on the new town ordered by Frederick William II. Then visit the Potsdam Film Museum (► 51) Alternatively take bus 695 from just beyond the Nauener Tor to Schloss Cecilienhof (► 25) or take the train to Babelsberg for a tour of the famous studios (► 59)

WALKS

THE SIGHTS

- New Synagogue (➤ 53)
- Monbijou Park (➤ 59)
- Sophienkirche (➤ 53)
- Elisabethkirche
- Volkspark am Weinberg
- Water-tower
- Käthe Kollwitz memorial
- Museum of Berlin Working-class Life (➤ 51)

INFORMATION

Distance 5km
Time 2½ hours
Start point Oranienburger Strasse
✚ J4
🚇 S-Bahn Oranienburger Strasse
End point Husemannstrasse
✚ K2
🚇 U-Bahn Eberswalder Strasse
🍴 Café: Café Oren (➤ 68); Restaurant: Restauration 1900 (➤ 63)

Café on Husemannstrasse

PRENZLAUER BERG AND THE SCHEUNENVIERTEL

Walk eastwards along Oranienburger Strasse, heart of the Scheunenviertel (Barn Quarter), which became the Jewish Quarter in the late 17th century. Dominating the skyline is the golden dome of the New Synagogue. Lower down, on the right, is Monbijou Park, once the grounds of a royal palace, and, on the left, the remains of the Old Jewish Cemetery, destroyed by the Nazis.

Turn left into Rosenthaler Strasse and then first left into Sophienstrasse. This neighbourhood is now an artists' enclave. Between Sophienstrasse and Oranienburger Strasse are the historic court-yards known as the Hackesche Höfe. These 19th-century workers' houses and factory work-shops are now smart restaurants, boutiques, art galleries and theatres.

Continue along Sophienstrasse, passing the 18th-century Sophienkirche, then follow Grosse Hamburger Strasse. No. 11, 'The Missing House', commemorates its occupants, who were all killed in an Allied bombing raid. Cross Koppenplatz into Ackerstrasse, the heart of an old working-class quarter.

On the opposite side of Invalidenstrasse are the remains of Schinkel's Elisabethkirche (1832). Walk east along Veteranenstrasse, past the Volkspark am Weinberg and join Kastanienallee briefly before turning right into Schwedter Strasse. Cross Senefelderplatz into Kollwitzstrasse. On the right, just off Belforter Strasse, is the 19th-century water-tower, used by the Nazis as a makeshift prison and torture chamber in 1933. At Kollwitzplatz is a memorial to the Expressionist artist Käthe Kollwitz.

Husemannstrasse has a lively café scene nowadays, but the refurbished tenement blocks disguise a more squalid past – the story is told in the Museum of Working-class Life.

SCHÖNEBERG

First mentioned in 1264 as Sconenberch, the residential quarter of Berlin now known as Schöneberg was not formally incorporated into the city until 1920.

Before you leave Wittenbergplatz station, take time to admire its art-deco interior, then walk down Kleiststrasse to Nollendorfplatz, the centre of twenties nightlife and still home to the Metropol, dating from 1906. Walk south along Maassenstrasse, crossing Nollendorfstrasse. British author Christopher Isherwood, whose reminiscences of Berlin life in the 1930s inspired the film *Cabaret*, lived here at Nollendorfstrasse 17. The next square you come to, Winterfeldtplatz, is best known for its twice-weekly market.

At the end of Maassenstrasse is Pallasstrasse; the Sportspalast which once stood here was the scene of many of Adolf Hitler's rallies. The flak tower nearby is a wartime survivor and was part of the city's defences.

Cross Pallasstrasse into Elssholzstrasse. On the left is Kleistpark, named after the German Romantic poet Heinrich von Kleist, who tragically shot himself on the shores of the Wannsee in 1811, aged only 34. Just inside the park is the former Supreme Court of Justice (Kammergericht), where Count von Stauffenberg and other instigators of the failed July Bomb Plot to assassinate Hitler were tried in 1944. Just a few months later the judge, the infamous Roland Freisler, was killed when the building sustained a direct hit during an Allied bombing raid.

Turn right into Grunewaldstrasse, then left into Martin-Luther-Strasse. Dominating John-F-Kennedy-Platz is the Rathaus Schöneberg, former town hall of West Berlin. It was from the balcony of this building that US President John F Kennedy delivered his famous 'Ich bin ein Berliner' speech on 26 June 1963, only months before his assassination.

THE SIGHTS

- Wittenbergplatz U-Bahn (➤ 60)
- Metropol Theater (➤ 78)
- Nollendorfstrasse 17
- Winterfeldtmarkt (➤ 75)
- Kleistpark
- Schöneberg Town Hall

INFORMATION

Distance 5km
Time 2½ hours
Start point Wittenbergplatz U-Bahn
🚇 F7
Ⓜ U-Bahn Wittenbergplatz
End point Rathaus Schöneberg
🚇 F9
Ⓜ U-Bahn Rathaus Schöneberg
🍴 Café: Tim's Canadian Deli (➤ 69); Restaurant: Haquin (➤ 66)

Plaque commemorating Kennedy's speech

EVENING STROLLS

"Stage in the Woods"

Warm summer evenings are perfect for a visit to the Waldbühne, Berlin's most famous open-air stage. Completed in 1936 and rediscovered in the 1980s, the Waldbühne hosts everything from rock concerts to film shows (► 82).

Savignyplatz

KREUZBERG

Emerge from the shadows of Görlitzer Bahnhof into the uneven glare of a typical Kreuzberg junction. The litter-strewn pavements, spray-painted walls and the sounds of the Orient are enlivened after dusk by a crazily vibrant night scene – pool halls, off-beat cafés, milk bars, all-night pubs and numerous cheap restaurants. Head north-west along Oranienstrasse to Heinrichplatz where you will find the welcoming café-bar Rote Harfe (► 80).

Further on, turn left into Adalbertstrasse and head for Kottbusser Tor. The night air at 'Kotti' is impregnated with the pungent odour of kebabs and onions sold at numerous Imbiss stands. There are more bars on Kottbusser Strasse, which leads down to the Landwehrkanal. See this night stroll as an appetiser. If you like the Kreuzberg flavour, come again and explore a little further afield: try Wiener Strasse, Dresdener Strasse, Manteuffelstrasse and Hasenheide.

SAVIGNYPLATZ

Berliners are notorious show-offs and un-ashamedly fond of enjoying themselves. You will find evidence of both these characteristics in the streets around Savignyplatz, which claims the city's highest concentration of café-bars and international restaurants. Cross the square into Carmerstrasse. At Steinplatz turn left into Goethestrasse, then left again into Grolmanstrasse to return to Savignyplatz.

The night zone extends south of Kantstrasse too, so walk westwards along Kantstrasse as far as Schlüterstrasse. Turn left, and left again into Mommsenstrasse, then make your way back to Savignyplatz via Knesebeckstrasse.

Bring the evening to an agreeable end with a drink in the Schwarzes Café (► 69).

ORGANISED SIGHTSEEING

CITY TOURS

BERLIN CITY CIRCLE (BVB)
City circle tour. Duration 2 hours. Also 1/2-day ticket for visitors wishing to hop on and off.
✉ Kurfürstendamm 225 ☎ 8859880

BERLIN TOURISMUS
Tours include Jewish Life and History, Entertainment, The Cold War, Capital in Transformation, Prussian Residences. ✉ Berlin Tourismus Marketing GmbH, Am Karlsbad 11 ☎ 26474853

BEROLINA SIGHTSEEING
Bus tours of Berlin and Potsdam-Sanssouci. Departures from Ku'damm.
✉ Meinekestrasse 3 ☎ 568030

BUS 100
The route from Zoo Station to Alexanderplatz takes in many of Berlin's main attractions. Departures from Zoo Station every 10 minutes.

WALKS

INSIDER TOUR
English-speaking Berliners give visitors an insider's view of the city. Duration 3 hours.
✉ Boppstrasse 3 ☎ 6923149

THE ORIGINAL BERLIN WALKS
'Discover Berlin' and 'Infamous Third Reich Sights' are the English-language tours on offer.
✉ Harbigstrasse 26 ☎ 3019194

OUT–OF–TOWN EXCURSIONS

SEVERIN AND KÜHN
Nightclub tour by coach, and tours to Dresden, Mark Brandenburg and the Spreewald.
✉ Kurfürstendamm 216 ☎ 8804190

BBS (Berliner Bären Stadtrundfahrt)
Coach tours to Potsdam, Dresden, the Spreewald.
✉ Rankestrasse 35 ☎ 35195270
✉ Alexanderplatz ☎ 2476870

Berlin by boat

Reederei Heinz Riedel
For an original view of Berlin, the round trip of canals and waterways offered by this steamboat company is hard to beat. Departures are from Kottbusser Brücke.
✉ Planufer 78
☎ 6913782

Stern und Kreisschiffahrt
Tours include the Havel, the city canals and the River Spree. Other destinations: Köpenick, Muggelsee and the Spreewald. Departure points: Tegel (Greenwich Prom.), Wannsee station, Jannowitzbrücke and Treptower Harbour.
✉ Puschkinallee 16
☎ 16173900

Yacht Charter
Hire an 18m yacht with friends for a luxury cruise on the Havel.
✉ Berliner Strasse 26–7, Potsdam
☎ 8214658

Excursions

INFORMATION

Bernau

🚈 From Schönhauser Allee or Friedrichstrasse (frequent trains; change at Bornholmer Strasse)

➕ Off map to northeast

Distance 36km northeast of Berlin

Journey time About 1 hour

Tourist Information
Berlin offices (▶ 93)

Lutherstadt Wittenberg

🚈 From Bahnhof Berlin-Lichtenberg (trains every hour)

➕ Off map to southwest

Distance 60km southwest of Berlin

Journey time About 1 hour

Tourist Information

✉ Collegienstrasse 28

☎ (03491) 2239/2537

Lübbenau

🚈 From Bahnhof Berlin-Lichtenberg (trains every 2 hours)

➕ Off map to southeast

Distance 70km southeast of Berlin

Journey time About 1½ hours

Tourist Information

✉ Poststrasse 25

☎ (03542) 2236/5887

BERNAU

Berlin is necklaced with attractive old villages of which Bernau is a fine example. Founded in 1232, even earlier than Berlin itself, Bernau has preserved its medieval heritage to a surprising extent. The robust city wall, all 1,500m of it, has kept its battlements and defences largely intact. Find out more about the history of Bernau at the local history museum, a monument in its own right located in the 14th-century Steintor. Also of interest are the 16th-century former grammar school, the Marienkirche and the 18th-century hangman's house.

LUTHERSTADT WITTENBERG

Wittenberg is famous throughout the world as the cradle of the Reformation, for it was here that an obscure monk named Martin Luther began a protest against the Roman Catholic Church that ended in his excommunication and the birth of Protestantism. The Lutherhaus, on Collegienstrasse in the former monastery where Luther later lived with his wife and family, is a wonderfully vivid museum of the German Reformation. The house of his friend and brother-in-arms, Philip Melanchthon, is also open to the public. The Castle Church, where in 1517 Luther nailed his 95 theses attacking the Church, is less interesting than the Stadtkirche, which has survived with many of its original features intact, including a beautiful altar panel by Lucas Cranach the Elder. He was not merely a painter but Wittenberg's wealthiest citizen and mayor; there are plans to open his studio, the Cranachhöfe, to the public.

LÜBBENAU

Lübbenau is an ideal launching pad for exploring the Spreewald, a scenic wonderland of lakes, canals, farmsteads and country inns. The Spreewaldmuseum is near the 19th-century Schloss. The houses around the Marktplatz are worthy examples of the late baroque as is the church (Stadtkirche St Nikolai). An attractive timber-framed building is the only reminder of the old town hall (Rathaus). Also interesting is a

Saxon mile-post dating from the 18th century. Lübbenau is an embarkation point for boat trips and has a small harbour.

BRANDENBURG

Dominsel is the charmingly understated focal point of the capital of Mark Brandenburg. It was here that the first Slav settlers arrived in the 6th century, later founding the Romanesque cathedral (Dom). This beautiful building survives in its 14th-century Gothic transformation and should not be missed. If this part of the town has a tranquil, almost forgotten air, the Old Town (Altstadt) is more closely attuned to the modern world although there are attractions here too, notably the market-place (Markt) with its late-Gothic town hall (Rathaus). The New Town (Neustadt) was founded in the late 12th century. There are plenty of shops and cafés in the pedestrianised zone, but the highlight is the Katherinenkirche in the market place, with its medieval sculptures and ceiling paintings. The countryside around Brandenburg is outstanding. Lake Beetzsee, where regattas often take place, is popular and accessible.

INFORMATION

Brandenburg

🚆 From Friedrichstrasse or Zoologischer Garten (trains every hour)

➕ Off map to west

Distance 62km west of Berlin

Journey time About 45 minutes

Tourist Information

✉ Hauptstrasse 51

☎ (03381) 23743

The Brandenburger Roland guards the late-Gothic town hall

WHAT'S ON

On any given day, Berlin may have 250 exhibitions, and there are over 400 independent theatre groups, 170 museums, 200 art galleries and more than 150 auditoriums. It's not surprising that Berlin's listing magazines (▶ 92) are among the fattest in Europe!

JANUARY	Traditional New Year celebrations at the Brandenburg Gate *6-Day Race* Event for cyclists, held in the Velodrom, Landsberger Allee
FEBRUARY	World-famous *International Film Festival*
MAY	*German Women's Open* Tennis tournament; at LTTC Rot Weiss in Grunewald
JUNE	*Fete de la Musique* Inter-cultural music *Christopher Street Day* Procession celebrating the lives of gays and lesbians
JULY	*Love Parade* 'The largest rave party in the world', with more than 1 million young people (especially fans of techno music) turning out
SEPTEMBER	*Berlin Arts Festival* Opera, music, theatre and arts events throughout the city
SEPTEMBER/OCTOBER	*Berlin Marathon*
OCTOBER	*German Unity Day* (3 October) See listings magazines for special events
NOVEMBER	Anniversary of opening of Berlin Wall (9 November)
DECEMBER	Special markets held during the Christmas season sell Christmas foods and decorations at regular venues, including Marx-Engels-Platz, Platz der Vereinten Nationen (Friedrichshain) and Breitscheidplatz. These characteristically German festive goods make unusual and welcome presents or souvenirs. The Dahlem Christmas Market (Königin-Luise-Strasse 49) offers traditional arts and crafts, games for children and carriage rides to Grunewald.

BERLIN's
top 25 sights

The sights are shown on the maps on the inside front cover and
inside back cover, numbered **1–25** from west to east across the city

1	Sanssouci	24
2	Cecilienhof	25
3	Klein-Glienicke	26
4	Spandau	27
5	Grunewald	28
6	Sachsenhausen Concentration Camp	29
7	Ethnographical Museum (Museum für Völkerkunde)	30
8	Schloss Charlottenburg	31
9	Kurfürstendamm	32
10	Kaiser Wilhelm Memorial Church (Gedächtniskirche)	33
11	Bauhaus Museum	34
12	Kulturforum	35
13	Museum of Applied Art (Kunstgewerbemuseum)	36
14	Tiergarten	37
15	Topography of Terror	38
16	Brandenburg Gate	39
17	Checkpoint Charlie	40
18	Gendarmenmarkt	41
19	Unter den Linden	42
20	Museums Island (Museumsinsel)	43
21	Pergamon Museum	44
22	Berlin Cathedral (Berliner Dom)	45
23	Nikolaiviertel	46
24	Alexanderplatz	47
25	Schloss Köpenick	48

1

SANSSOUCI

Frederick the Great's Sanssouci was to be a residence where the Prussian monarch could 'get away from it all', a place of carefree relaxation but also of peaceful seclusion. For us, the charmingly eccentric Chinese Teahouse epitomises his ideal.

HIGHLIGHTS

- Schloss Sanssouci
- Terraces and Great Fountain
- Grave of Frederick the Great
- Neptune grotto
- Orangery
- Friedenskirche
- Sicilian gardens
- Roman Baths (Römische Bäder)
- New Palace
- Ape bearing Voltaire's features, on the Chinese Teahouse

INFORMATION

- ✚ Off map to southwest
- ✉ Zur historischen Mühle, Potsdam
- ☎ (0331) 9694202
- ◷ Schloss Sanssouci: Apr–Oct Tue–Sun 9–5. Nov–Mar Tue–Sun 9–3. Closed Mon New Palace: Apr–Oct Wed–Mon 9–5. Nov–Mar Wed–Mon 9–3. Closed Tue
- 🍴 Café (£); restaurant (££)
- 🚇 S-Bahn Potsdam Stadt
- 🚌 Bus 606, 610, 695
- 🚏 Wild Park
- ♿ None
- 🎫 Park: free
  Schloss: expensive (with guided tour)
  New Palace: moderate
- ↔ Cecilienhof (► 25)

The landscaped expanse of Sanssouci Park, on the western fringes of Potsdam, contains not one but two quite different, but equally impressive, palaces built for Frederick the Great. Formal gardens, terraces, fountains and follies complete the picture. Don't be put off by the crowds milling around Schloss Sanssouci. The other sights and the grounds are much less congested.

Schloss Sanssouci Frederick's celebrated retreat was designed by a personal friend of his, Georg Wenzeslaus von Knobelsdorff. The single-storey rococo façade, topped by a shallow green dome, conceals a succession of gorgeously furnished rooms and a collection of precious objects including sculptures, painted vases and elaborate clocks. The French philosopher Voltaire was Sanssouci's most famous guest – he eventually fell out with Frederick, who said disparagingly 'he has the slyness and will of an ape'.

New Palace If Sanssouci is the perfect illustration of Frederick the Great's cultivated side, then the New Palace (Neues Palais) reveals his obsession with self-aggrandisement. The best view of the expansive redbrick façade is from the imposing driveway, surely intended both to intimidate and impress courtiers and foreign visitors alike. Johann Büring designed the exterior and Karl von Gontard the sumptuous interior. Unfortunately many of the rooms appear dilapidated owing to long-term neglect, although restoration work is in progress.

CECILIENHOF

A trip to Potsdam Town (rewarding in itself) can easily be combined with a short excursion to this unusual palace which played host to the inter-Allied Potsdam Conference in 1945.

Potsdam Conference Set just north of Potsdam in an area of parkland called the Neuer Garten, Schloss Cecilienhof was the setting for the last great inter-Allied government conference of World War II. Convened in July 1945 as Berlin and its environs lay in ruins, the avowed purpose of this summit was to redraw the post-war map of Europe. The leading delegates were the so-called 'Big Three': Winston Churchill, representing Great Britain, Harry S Truman of the United States and, heading the Soviet delegation, Josef Stalin. Visitors can see the conference hall itself and the studies and reception rooms of the various delegations.

Palace and grounds Schloss Cecilienhof's other distinguished resident was Kaiser Wilhelm II, who commissioned this semi-rural retreat in the style of an English country house, ironically during World War I. The Hohenzollerns occupied the palace until 1945.

Much older than the palace itself are the buildings in the grounds, notably the Marmorpalais, conceived by Karl von Gontard in 1787–9. Vines used to grow here in abundance – there were more than 40 vineyards in the 18th century. The Dutch-style servants' quarters mirror the celebrated Dutch Quarter in Potsdam Town. Also of interest are the original garden houses, orangery and the ruined library.

HIGHLIGHTS

- Conference table
- Offices of the three powers
- Tudor-style chimneys
- Marmorpalais
- Ruined library
- Shingle House
- Carved oak staircase
- Sphinx on the Orangery

INFORMATION

- ✚ Off map to southwest
- ✉ Neuer Garten
- ☎ (0331) 9694202
- ⏰ Tue–Sun 9–5. Closed Mon
- 🍽 Restaurant (£££)
- Ⓢ S-Bahn Potsdam-Stadt
- 🚌 Bus 695
- Potsdam-Stadt
- ♿ None
- Moderate
- ↔ Sanssouci (➤ 24)

Cecilienhof's 'Tudor' chimneys

25

3

KLEIN-GLIENICKE

HIGHLIGHTS

- Ornamental gardens
- Lion fountain
- Casino with pergolas
- Relics from the Temple of Poseidon
- Rotunda (Grosse Neugierde)
- Teahouse (Kleine Neugierde)
- Stibadium, pavilion
- Klosterhof
- Glienicker Bridge
- View of Havel

INFORMATION

- Off map to southwest
- Königstrasse 36
- 8053041
- Park: dawn to dusk daily
  Schloss: not open
- Excellent restaurant (£££)
- S-Bahn Wannsee
- Bus 93, 116
- Potsdam-Stadt
- None
- Free
- Cecilienhof (➤ 25)

The park surrounding this elegant villa and former royal residence is perched decoratively on the banks of the Jungfernsee (Havel). Just outside the park gate is the Glienicker Bridge, which was famous as a setting for Cold War spy novels.

The Schloss and park The mock-Renaissance Schloss (not open) was designed in 1824 for the brother of Kaiser Wilhelm I, Prince Friedrich Karl of Prussia, by Karl Friedrich Schinkel. Nowadays the grounds are famous for their arcadian follies and ornamental gardens: the follies are by Schinkel, while the park was laid out by Peter Lenné (also responsible for the Berlin Tiergarten). Looking for rhyme or reason in the choice of follies is in the end a fruitless exercise although the themes of Renaissance Italy and Classical Greece can be detected here and there. The most extraordinary flight of fancy must be the Klosterhof. For once these remains are genuinely Italian: the cloister came from a monastery near Venice, while the capital decorated with the chained monkey once belonged to Pisa's famous Leaning Tower.

Glienicker Bridge (Glienicker Brücke) Just outside the gate is the Glienicker Bridge, which spans the Havel at the southern end of the Jungfernsee to link Berlin with Potsdam. Unremarkable in itself, the bridge came to the world's attention in 1962 when, marking the border between East and West, it was the scene of a spy swap involving the American pilot, Gary Powers, who had recently been shot down by the Soviet air force in the famous 'U-2 incident'. The bridge subsequently starred in films and spy novels and became a symbol of the Cold War.

SPANDAU

Of the many attractive villages on Berlin's outskirts, a favourite is ancient Spandau with its redbrick fortress (Zitadelle), picturesque streets and views across the Havel. The best vantage point is the Juliusturm, the oldest surviving part of the Zitadelle.

The Zitadelle Spandau became important in the Middle Ages, thanks to its strategic location at the confluence of the rivers Spree and Havel. The first Zitadelle, dating from the 12th century, was rebuilt by Joachim III in 1557. The oldest surviving part of the building is the crenellated Juliusturm – the view from the top of the tower is worth the steep climb. Most of the bastions and out-buildings are 19th-century, though not the Old Magazine, which is as ancient as the castle itself.

Spandau castle was once famous as a cannon foundry. One exhibit is an 1860 model, recently brought back from remotest Siberia, where it had languished for more than a century. The fortress last saw active service during the Napoleonic Wars when the Old Arsenal was reduced to ruins. Just inside the gateway of the castle is the statue of a defiant Albrecht, the famous Bear of Brandenburg.

Altstadt Spandau Only a short walk from the castle is the attractive Old Town (Altstadt Spandau). The highlights are the Gothic house (Gotisches Haus) in Breite Strasse, dating from 1232, and the central square, Reformationsplatz, where you will find cafés and the Nikolaikirche. North of here lies the quaint old area known as the Kolk, and close by is Spandau's busy lock on the Havel.

HIGHLIGHTS

- Cannons
- Statue of Albrecht the Bear
- Museum of the Middle Ages
- Juliusturm
- Bastion walls
- Old Magazine
- Ruined arsenal
- Moat
- View from the Juliusturm
- Gothic house
- Kolk and Spandau lock

INFORMATION

- Off map to west
- Am Juliusturm
- 3391200
- Tue–Fri 9–5; Sat–Sun 10–5
- Am Juliusturm (£££) (► 62)
- U-Bahn Zitadelle
- Bus 133
- Spandau
- Few
- Moderate

Detail on the Zitadelle

5

GRUNEWALD

The Grunewald forest is an amazing tract of woodland on the western edge of the city. The dreamily scenic 32sq km, including lakes, beaches and nature reserves, are especially popular with Berliners at weekends.

HIGHLIGHTS

Jagdschloss Grunewald
● Hunting museum
● *Adam and Eve and Judith*, Lucas Cranach the Elder
● *Susannah and the Elders*, Jacob Jordaens
● *Julius Caesar*, Rubens
● Wooden ceiling in Great Hall
● *Trompe-l'oeil* stonework
● Antler candelabra
● Hexagonal stair turret

Grunewald Forest
● Grunewaldsee
● Grunewaldturm

INFORMATION

Jagdschloss Grunewald
✚ Off map to west
✉ Hüttenweg 100
☎ 8133597
◉ Apr–Sep Tue–Sun 10–1, 1:30–5. Oct–Mar Sat and Sun only
🍴 None
🚌 Bus 115, 183
♿ None
♿ Inexpensive
↔ Brücke Museum (► 52)

Grunewaldturm
✚ Off map to west
✉ Havelchaussee 61
☎ 3041203
◉ Tower: daily 10AM–dark
🍴 Café (£) ◉ Daily 11–11
🚌 Bus 218
♿ None
♿ Inexpensive

Hunting lodge Jagdschloss Grunewald is an attractive Renaissance hunting lodge, built in 1542 for Elector Joachim II of Brandenburg. The stables and outbuildings date from around 1700, when the house was surrounded by a moat. Today the lodge is a museum decorated with paintings and furniture from various royal collections; the chase is the predominant theme. One picture shows Kaiser Wilhelm on a visit to the Grunewald. The 17th-century Dutch school is well represented among the paintings on display, but the best work is by a German, Lucas Cranach the Elder, who has an entire room to himself. Equally remarkable is the painted wooden ceiling of the Great Hall (Grosser Saal) on the ground floor. This is the only surviving 16th-century room. Across the courtyard, the barn has been converted into a hunting museum.

Grunewald Forest Largely replanted with native trees following post-war felling for fuel, the forest offers pleasant walks, beaches fringing the Havel, and space for a host of leisure pursuits from boating to hang-gliding. The hunting lodge graces the shores of the Grunewaldsee, which is good for swimming. An alternative is the Krumme Lanke. Between these two lakes is a marshy nature reserve known as the Langes Luch. For views, climb the Grunewaldturm, a 78m folly on the banks of the Havel, built for Kaiser Wilhelm II in 1897. A second vantage point is the Teufelsberg (Devil's Mountain), an artificial hill made from wartime rubble.

SACHSENHAUSEN CONCENTRATION CAMP

Sachsenhausen concentration camp has been preserved as a memorial to the 100,000 prisoners who perished there during World War II. The buildings and their displays are a chilling reminder of the deception and evil once practised here, epitomised by the great lie 'Work makes you free' inscribed on the entrance gate.

INFORMATION

- Off map to northwest
- Strasse der Nationen
- (03301) 803719
- Apr–Sep Tue–Sun 8–6. Oct–Mar Tue–Sun 9–4:30
- None
- S-Bahn Oranienburg (then 20-minute walk)
- None
- Oranienburg
- Few
- Free

Nerve centre The Nazis opened the camp in July 1936, just as Berlin was preparing to host the Olympic Games. Sachsenhausen was the headquarters of the concentration camp inspectorate, and there was a training school here too.

Museums The two museums tell the terrible story of the camp: one focuses especially on the plight of the Jews; the other, in the former kitchens, displays various artefacts and other illustrations

Sachsenhausen today

of daily life. Some of the cells in the cell block have been restored in memory of heroes of the German and international resistance to Fascism. Outside are three wooden execution posts.

Extermination Camp Two of the original prison huts have been preserved, as well as the perimeter walls, fences and watch-towers. 'Station Z', where prisoners were exterminated before their bodies were cremated, occupies one corner of the site. The furnishings of the pathology department have been preserved, and also the tiled walls. Here corpses were dissected for experimental purposes. Films on various aspects of camp history are shown in the former laundry.

7

ETHNOGRAPHICAL MUSEUM

HIGHLIGHTS

- Polynesian clubhouse
- Oceanian boats
- Pre-Columbian gold statuettes
- Peruvian pottery
- Throne and footstool from Cameroon
- Benin bronzes
- Indonesian shadow puppets
- Sri Lankan carved masks
- Australian bark painting
- World music headphones

INFORMATION

- ✚ Off map to south
- ✉ Lansstrasse 8
- ☎ 83011
- ◐ Tue–Fri 9–5; Sat–Sun 10–5
- 🍽 Café (£)
- Ⓤ U-Bahn Dahlem-Dorf
- 🚌 Bus 183
- 🚉 Lichterfelde West
- ♿ Good
- 👜 Moderate
- ↔ Other Dahlem museums (➤ 51), Botanical Garden (➤ 56)

The folk art theme extends beyond the museum to Dahlem-Dorf U-Bahn station, where modern primitivist sculptures on the platform offer a provocative seating experience. Test them for comfort, then make your own artistic judgement.

Exhibitions Although the airy rooms of the Museum für Völkerkunde appear large, there is exhibition space for only a fraction of its 400,000-plus ethnographic items. For the time being, only Oceania and the Americas are represented by permanent exhibitions, while Africa, East Asia and South Asia feature in temporary displays.

Oceania The Oceanian boats are probably the highlight of the collection. The display includes an 18th-century vessel, known as a Tongiaki and resembling a catamaran, from the island of Tonga. For landlubbers there is the fantastically decorated male clubhouse, originating in the Palau Islands of the western Pacific.

Pre-Columbian art The focus of the American collection is the exhibition of ancient sculptures and figurines, mainly from Mexico and Peru.

Gold was the medium favoured by many of these artists and the craftsmanship represented here is perhaps among the best of its kind in the world. Just as beautiful, and more arresting, are the decorated stone *steles* from Cozumalhuapa (Guatemala) created to fend off evil spirits.

Mayan carvings

SCHLOSS CHARLOTTENBURG

This attractive former royal palace, built in the rococo style, lies in its own grounds only a stone's throw from the heart of Berlin. The highlights of the Schloss itself have to be the gorgeous White Hall and Golden Gallery, in the New Wing.

Royal retreat The Schloss was built over a period of more than 100 years and its development mirrors the aggrandisement of the Prussian dynasty of Hohenzollern, recalled in the forecourt by Andreas Schlüter's superb equestrian statue of the Great Elector, which once stood outside the Berlin Schloss. The Electress Sophie Charlotte's rural retreat, designed by Arnold Nering in 1695, was transformed into the palace we see today during the reigns of Frederick I and Frederick II by the architect Georg Wenzeslaus von Knobelsdorff. The Great Orangery and Theatre, and the Galerie der Romantik (which houses an exhibition of German Romantic painting) form wings of the Palace, as does the Langhans Building, now the Museum of Pre- and Early History.

Riverside grounds Do not leave Schloss Charlottenburg without seeing the delightful grounds which slope towards the River Spree. The formal French garden is a marked contrast to the landscaped English garden, in which will be found the Mausoleum, built for Queen Luise, and the Belvedere, now a museum devoted to Berlin porcelain, a famous product of the city. Closer to the palace, do not miss the delightfully idiosyncratic Pavilion, designed by Berlin's best-known 19th-century architect, Karl Friedrich Schinkel.

HIGHLIGHTS

- White Hall
- Golden Gallery
- Gobelins rooms
- Study and bedchamber of Frederick I
- Galerie der Romantik
- *Embarkation for Cythera*, J-A Watteau (*above*)
- Statue of the Great Elector
- Schinkel Pavilion
- Great Orangery
- Gardens

A familiar landmark

INFORMATION

- ✛ B5
- ✉ Charlottenburg, Luisenplatz
- ☎ Schloss: 320911. Galerie der Romantik: 32091207
- ◷ Tue–Fri 9–5; Sat–Sun 10–5
- 🍴 Restaurant (££)
- Ⓤ U-Bahn Richard-Wagner-Platz
- 🚌 Bus 109, 110, 121, 145
- ♿ Few
- Moderate
- ↔ Bröhan Museum (► 50), Egyptian Museum (► 51)

31

9

KURFÜRSTENDAMM

HIGHLIGHTS

- Literaturhaus
- Käthe Kollwitz Museum
- Wertheim department store
  (➤ 70)
- Café Möhring (➤ 68)
- Café Kranzler (➤ 68)
- Fasanenstrasse
- Iduna House
- Bristol Hotel Kempinski
  (➤ 84)
- Neo-classical news-stands

INFORMATION

➕ E7
🚇 U-Bahn Uhlandstrasse
🚌 Bus 109, 119, 129, 219
🚉 Zoologischer Garten
↔ Kaiser Wilhelm Memorial
Church (➤ 33)

**Literaturhaus and
Wintergarten Café**
✉ Fasanenstrasse 23
☎ 8825414
🕐 Daily 10AM–1AM
🍴 Excellent (££)
♿ Few
♻ Free

Käthe Kollwitz Museum
✉ Fasanenstrasse 24
☎ 8825210
🕐 Wed–Mon 11–6
♿ Few
♻ Moderate

It would be perverse to spend more than a day or two in Berlin without visiting the Ku'damm. Berlin's famous tree-lined boulevard has numerous pavement cafés and restaurants, in addition to all the city's major shops.

Shopping street The Ku'damm stretches for nearly 3.5km towards Charlottenburg. Many of its stores are the beneficiaries of the *Wirtschaftswunder*, the economic miracle of the 1960s brought about partly by American investment.

New West End The elegant streets off the Ku'damm (Fasanenstrasse, for example) were a part of the New West End, developed as a residential area at the end of the 19th century. Many of the houses here are now commercial art galleries; an exception is the museum devoted to the life and work of the 20th-century artist Käthe Kollwitz (Fasanenstrasse 24). Next door to this museum is the Literaturhaus, a cultural centre with a secluded garden café, the Wintergarten. The Villa Grisebach at no. 25 is an outstanding example of Jugendstil architecture. A little further away (on the corner of Leibnizstrasse) is another period piece, the Iduna House, whose unmistakable cupola dates from 1907.

Coffee shops The café tradition in Berlin has been preserved in the old names of Kranzler and Möhring. Johann Georg Kranzler opened the first coffee shop in Berlin in 1835, although the original site was on the corner of Friedrichstrasse. Tourists and literati have taken the place of the Prussian aristocracy; join them for a while to rest your legs, enjoy a superb coffee and watch the world go by.

10

KAISER WILHELM MEMORIAL CHURCH

The blackened ruin of the Gedächtnis-kirche in Breitscheidplatz − a reminder of the futility of war − casts a shadow over the Ku'damm's sunny commercialism. Particularly moving is the cross of nails given by the people of Coventry, England—another war-torn city.

War memorial The memorial church was Kaiser Wilhelm II's contribution to the developing New West End. Built in 1895 in Romanesque style, it was always rather incongruous in this proudly modern section of the city. No expense was spared on the interior, its dazzling mosaics deliberately reminiscent of St Mark's in Venice. When Allied bombs destroyed the church in 1943, the shell was allowed to stand. Poignant in its way, the old building now serves as a small museum focusing on the wartime destruction.

The New Chapel The octagonal chapel and hexagonal stained-glass tower, both uncompromisingly modern, have been denigrated by Berliners (the 'make-up box' and the 'lipstick tube' are the favoured nicknames). However, many visitors find peace in the blue-hued chapel (stained glass from Chartres, France), designed by Egon Eiermann in the early 1960s.

Breitscheidplatz In shameless contrast, brash Breitscheidplatz proclaims the values of a materialistic, throwaway culture, only partially redeemed by the colourful buskers and occasional fund-raising stunts. Nowadays it is a refuge for Berlin's down-and-outs, routinely targeted by the police. The focus is the Globe Fountain (Weltkugelbrunnen).

HIGHLIGHTS

- Cross of nails
- Surviving mosaics
- Models of city centre
- The Stalingrad Madonna
- Bell-tower
- Globe Fountain

INFORMATION

- E6
- Breitscheidplatz
- 2185023
- Memorial Hall Museum:
  Tue–Sat 10–4
  New Chapel: 9–7
- U- or S-Bahn Zoologischer
  Garten, Kurfürstendamm
- Bus 100, 119, 129, 146
- Zoologischer Garten
- Few
- Free
- Kurfürstendamm (➤ 32),
  Tiergarten (➤ 37),
  Europa–Center (➤ 76)

Breitscheidplatz

33

11

BAUHAUS MUSEUM

HIGHLIGHTS

- Walter Gropius's building
- Marcel Breuer's leather armchair
- Metal-framed furniture
- Ceramics
- Moholy-Nagy's sculpture *Light-space-modulator*
- Designs and models of Bauhaus buildings
- Paintings by Paul Klee
- Paintings by Kandinsky
- Schlemmer's theatre designs
- Marianne Brandt's tea and coffee set

INFORMATION

- F6
- Klingelhöferstrasse 14
- 2540020
- Wed–Mon 10–5
- Café (£)
- U-Bahn Nollendorfplatz
- Bus 100, 129, 187, 341
- Bellevue
- Good
- Moderate
- Kulturforum (➤ 35), Tiergarten (➤ 37)

Brush up on your knowledge of the history of design by visiting one of Berlin's foremost cultural totems. The exhibition in the Bauhaus celebrates one of the most influential art and design movements of the 20th century.

Bauhaus In the traumatic aftermath of World War I all values, artistic ones included, came under scrutiny. In Germany, the dynamic outcome was the Bauhaus school, founded in 1919 by Walter Gropius in Weimar, the capital of the recently founded Republic. Gropius and his disciples stressed function, rather than decoration, in architecture and design, favouring modern materials such as concrete and tubular steel for their versatility and appearance.

Mass-production guaranteed the Bauhaus an unprecedented influence on European and transatlantic architecture and design. Most remarkable, perhaps, was the school's insistence on collaboration between different artistic disciplines. Workshops in metalwork, print and advertising, photography, painting and ceramics were loosely co-ordinated by a cohort of outstanding team leaders, among them Vassily Kandinsky, Paul Klee, Oskar Schlemmer and Laszlo Moholy-Nagy.

Legacy Almost inevitably the revolutionary credentials of the Bauhaus drove it into conflict with the Nazis. Already forced to move to Dessau and then to Berlin, the school was closed in 1933. But its influence lives on in the design of furniture and appliances found in countless 20th-century homes.

The exhibition is housed in a purpose-built museum designed by Walter Gropius in 1964.

KULTURFORUM

A complex of galleries, museums and concert halls, conceived in the 1960s by Hans Scharoun, the Kulturforum is controversial as architecture. But no one disputes the beauty of the collections in the Gemäldegalerie and the New National Gallery. Don't miss them.

Gemäldegalerie (Picture Gallery) Comprising European painting of the 13th–18th centuries and only recently moved here from Dahlem, the Gemäldegalerie stands out for its northern European medieval and Renaissance art. German masters, including Dürer, Hans Holbein and Lucas Cranach the Elder, are well represented, as are the great Dutch artists, Van Eyck, Rogier van der Weyden and Pieter Bruegel. Dutch baroque painting is also prominent, with several outstanding works by Rembrandt, among others. The Italian collection reads like a roll-call of great Renaissance artists: Fra Angelico, Piero della Francesco, Giovanni Bellini and Raphael.

The New National Gallery Designed by Bauhaus architect Mies van der Rohe for the hanging of large canvasses, the Neue Nationalgalerie concentrates on international modern art. Many leading post-war artists are represented here – Robert Rauschenberg, Roy Lichtenstein, Frank Stella, Joseph Beuys. The lower floor displays work by 20th-century Europeans, including Kirchner, Magritte, Klee, Max Ernst, Otto Dix, de Chirico, Dalí, Picasso.

Museum of Musical Instruments There is everything here, from bagpipes to synthesisers. The policy is strictly 'no touch', but you can hear tapes of the instruments in performance on strategically placed headphones.

HIGHLIGHTS

Gemäldegalerie
- *Netherlandish Proverbs*, Pieter Bruegel
- *Portrait of Enthroned Madonna and Child*, Botticelli
- *Portrait of Georg Gisze*, Rembrandt

New National Gallery
- *Pillars of Society*, George Grosz
- *Departure of the Ships*, Paul Klee
- *L'Idée Fixe*, René Magritte
- *The Archer*, Henry Moore (in the sculpture park)

Museum of Musical Instruments
- Orchestron organ
- World's first bass tuba

INFORMATION

✚ G6
✉ Potsdamer Strasse 50
☎ New National Gallery: 2662662
Museum of Musical Instruments: 254810
🕐 Tue–Fri 9–5; Sat–Sun 10–5
🍴 Cafés ($$)
Ⓤ U-Bahn Kurfürstenstrasse
🚌 Bus 129, 148, 248, 348
♿ Good
🎫 Moderate; additional charge for temporary exhibitions in New National Gallery
↔ Bauhaus Museum (► 34), Museum of Applied Art (► 36), Tiergarten (► 37)

13

MUSEUM OF APPLIED ART

HIGHLIGHTS

- 8th-century Burse reliquary
- Frederick Barbarossa's baptismal bowl
- J J Kaendler's Harlequin Group
- Lidded goblet of gold ruby glass from Potsdam
- Lüneburg silver
- Gold elephant fountain from Koln
- Guelph reliquary from Koln
- Majolica love dish from Urbino
- Art-deco stained-glass windows
- 'Wiggle-chair' by Frank Gehry

INFORMATION

- ✚ G6
- ✉ Tiergartenstrasse 6
- ☎ 2662911
- ◷ Tue–Fri 9–5; Sat–Sun 10–5
- 🍴 Café (£)
- 🚇 U-Bahn Kurfürstenstrasse
- 🚌 Bus 129, 148, 187, 248, 341
- ♿ Good
- 💷 Inexpensive
- ↔ Bauhaus Museum (➤ 34), Kulturforum (➤ 35), Tiergarten (➤ 37)

Berlin's wonderful collection of arts and crafts is in the Museum of Applied Art housed in the Kulturforum. Pride of place belongs to the 8th-century Burse reliquary of Enger, an enamelled wooden box inlaid with gold and studded with silver, pearls and precious gems.

Cultural riches The vast exhibition is arranged chronologically on several floors. Every conceivable kind of applied art is accommodated including gold and silver work, glassware, majolica, jewellery, porcelain, furniture and clothing. A counterpoint to the exquisite medieval treasures assembled from churches and abbeys all over Germany is the Lüneburg Town Hall silver, evidence of the great wealth acquired by the burghers of the Hanseatic town in the 15th and 16th centuries.

Kunstkammer The museum is founded on the 7,000 objects acquired by the Brandenburg Kunstkammer (Cabinet of Curiosities) from the 17th century onwards. An intriguing item is the Pommersche Kunstschrank, an eclectic treasure-trove of objects from surgical instruments to hairbrushes and miniature books. It was assembled in 1610–16 for the Duke of Pommern-Stettin.

Porcelain and art deco Painted figurines from Meissen are the highlight of the porcelain collection. The Jugendstil glass, ceramics and jewellery are a feast for the eye – look out for the intricate ornamental fastener made by Lalique around 1900. On the ground floor is a display of art-deco furniture.

Porcelain figure of 1780

14

TIERGARTEN

Boating, strolling, jogging, summer concerts, ornamental gardens – this enormous (212ha) park right in the centre of Berlin offers all this and more. Look out for the antique gas lamps from various European cities along the route from the station to the Landwehrkanal.

Hunting ground *Tiergarten* means 'animal garden', recalling a time when the park was stocked with wild boar and deer for the convenience of the Prussian aristocracy. It was landscaped by Peter Joseph Lenné in the 1830s and still bears his imprint – remarkably, since the park was almost totally destroyed in World War II.

Siegessäule The victory column or Siegessäule occupies a prime site on Strasse des 17 Juni, although it originally stood in front of the Reichstag. Erected in 1873 to commemorate Prussian victories against Denmark, Austria and France, the 67m column is decorated with captured cannon. Beloved of Berliners is 'Gold Else', the victory goddess on the summit, waving her laurel wreath cheekily towards Paris.

War heroes and revolutionaries The three heroes of the Wars of Unification – Count Otto von Bismarck and Generals Helmut von Moltke and Albrecht von Roon – are all fêted with statues to the north of the Siegessäule. Memorials to two prominent revolutionaries, Karl Liebknecht and Rosa Luxemburg, stand beside the Landwehrkanal near Lichtensteinallee. Their bodies were dumped in the canal in 1919 by members of the right-wing Free Corps who had shot them shortly after an abortive Communist uprising.

HIGHLIGHTS

- Zoo and Aquarium (➤ 59)
- Kongresshalle
- Carillon
- Bismarck monument
- Schloss Bellevue
- 'Gold Else'
- Neuer See
- English Garden
- Soviet War Memorial
- Gas lamp collection

INFORMATION

Siegessäule
- ▦ F5
- ✉ Grosser Stern, Strasse des 17 Juni
- 🕐 Tue–Sun 9–6; Mon 1–6 (admission until 5:30)
- 🚇 S-Bahn Tiergarten
- 🚌 Bus 100
- ♿ None
- 💰 Inexpensive
- ↔ Bauhaus Museum (➤ 34), Kulturforum (➤ 35),
- ❓ Viewing platform (no lift)

The Siegessäule

37

TOPOGRAPHY OF TERROR

INFORMATION

➕ N6
✉ Stresemannstrasse 110
☎ 25486703
🕐 Daily 10–6
🚇 U-Bahn Kochstrasse, S-Bahn Anhalter Bahnhof
🚌 Bus 129, 341
🚆 Yorckstrasse
♿ None
🖐 Free
↔ Checkpoint Charlie (➤ 40)

Hardly a conventional tourist attraction, the Topographie des Terrors is an interpretive exhibition on the site of Hitler's Gestapo (Secret Police) headquarters. It gives solemn insights into the workings of the Führer's administration.

Exhibition An exhibition of photographs chronicling the rise of the Nazi terror regime, its functioning and its catastrophic demise is housed over the former SS kitchens and canteen. Next door was a hotel (used as offices) and, adjoining it, the stately Prinz-Albrecht-Palais, which faced on to Wilhelmstrasse. It was this building, known as Prinz-Albrecht-Strasse 8, that became 'the most feared address in Berlin'. Here, prisoners of the Third Reich, including members of the resistance, were interrogated and tortured, and from here the apparatus of oppression was administered with an eerie, bureaucratic efficiency. Outside the exhibition hall, beneath a canopy, are the foundations of the cells where prisoners were held, tortured and sometimes driven to suicide.

Topography A short distance away, a viewing platform resting on a mound of rubble gives a panoramic view of the entire Government Quarter (Regierungsviertel) between Unter den Linden and the Anhalter Bahnhof, where the various ministries of the Third Reich were located. With the help of photo-boards, visitors can place the Prinz-Albrecht-Palais, the former Air Ministry (still standing), the headquarters of Hitler's stormtroopers and the offices of the propaganda newspaper *Der Angriff*. It is sobering to contemplate the size and complexity of Hitler's administrative organisation, and to stand on the site where so many atrocities were committed.

BRANDENBURG GATE

The Brandenburg Gate began life as a humble toll-gate, marking the city's western boundary. Today it symbolises the recent reconciliation of East and West and has even been used as a backdrop for celebratory events – and for pop concerts.

Gate of Peace? The Gate is the work of Karl Gotthard Langhans and dates from 1788–91. Its neo-classical style echoes the ancient entrance to the Acropolis in Athens on which it is modelled. Originally conceived as an Arch of Peace, the Brandenburg Gate has more frequently been used to glorify martial values, as in 1933 when the Nazis' torchlight procession through the arch was intended to mark the beginning of the 1,000-year Reich.

Viktoria *The Quadriga*, a sculpture depicting the goddess Viktoria driving her chariot, was added to the gate by Johann Gottfried Schadow in 1794. In 1806, following the Prussian defeat at Jena, it was removed to Paris by Napoleon. When it was brought back in triumph less than a decade later, Karl Friedrich Schinkel added a wreath of oak leaves and the original iron cross to Viktoria's standard. During the heyday of cabaret in the 1920s, *The Quadriga* was frequently parodied by scantily clad chorus girls.

Pariser Platz The rebuilding of this famous square is now well under way. The Adlon Hotel, one of the most luxurious in Europe, opened in 1997. By 2000, the US, British and French embassies will also be here.

INFORMATION

- *The Quadriga*
- Classical reliefs
- Pock-marks from shrapnel damage
- Adjoining classical pavilions
- View down Unter den Linden
- View down Strasse des 17 Juni
- *The Crier* statue by Gerhard Marcks
- Pariser Platz
- Daimler-Benz building site

The Quadriga

INFORMATION

- H5
- Pariser Platz
- S-Bahn Unter den Linden, U-Bahn Französische Strasse
- Bus 100
- Friedrichstrasse
- None
- Free
- Tiergarten (➤ 37), Unter den Linden (➤ 42), Reichstag (➤ 55)

39

17

CHECKPOINT CHARLIE

HIGHLIGHTS

- Site of barrier
- Top of watch-tower
- Memorial to Wall victim
- Four-language sign

Haus am Checkpoint Charlie
- Wall graffiti exhibition
- Isetta car
- Hot-air balloon
- Fragment of Wall
- Story of life in a divided city

INFORMATION

- ✚ J6
- ✉ Friedrichstrasse 43–4
- ☎ 2511031
- 🕐 Daily 9AM–10PM
- 🍴 Café (£)
- Ⓤ U-Bahn Kochstrasse
- 🚌 Bus 129
- Ⓡ Yorckstrasse
- ♿ None
- Ⓔ Expensive
- ↔ Topography of Terror
  (➤ 38)

❝Berlin will be famous for its Wall long after Berliners have consigned it to memory. The museum in the Haus am Checkpoint Charlie offers a colourful, if highly commercialised, presentation of the Wall experience.❞

Border Crossing Though its name will doubtless live on for some time to come, triggering memories of the Cold War, the original hut at Checkpoint Charlie was dismantled in 1990 and removed to a museum. All that remains is the red and white barrier and the sign (in English, French, German and Russian) warning 'You are now leaving the American Sector'.

Confrontation It was at Checkpoint Charlie that Soviet and US tanks confronted one another in October 1961 at the height of the Cold War. A new complex of offices and shops has now replaced the buildings of this most famous of border crossings. Close by, a fenced-off section contains a motley collection of Wall paraphernalia including sentry boxes, chevron posts, booby traps, rolls of barbed wire and pieces of wall. Vendors sell mementoes near by.

Haus am Checkpoint Charlie The museum is popular with backpackers and young people generally, and often gets crowded. On display are adapted vehicles, trick suitcases, a hot-air balloon and other contraptions used by refugees making their escape to the West. This emphasis on the sensational sits uncomfortably with the museum's stated purpose which is to remind visitors of the broader human rights implications of the Wall. There are exhibitions using film and video on the history of the Wall, on painters and graffiti artists, and on the non-violent struggle for human rights, from Gandhi to Lech Walesa.

GENDARMENMARKT

This beautiful square comes as a pleasant surprise for visitors who associate Berlin with imperial bombast and Prussian marching bands. Climb the tower of the Französischer Dom for superb views of the Friedrichstadt.

Konzerthaus Known originally as the Schauspielhaus (theatre), the Konzerthaus was designed by Karl Friedrich Schinkel in 1821. Its predecessor had been destroyed by fire during a rehearsal of Schiller's play *The Robbers* so it is fitting that the playwright's monument stands outside. When the building was restored in the early 1980s after being severely damaged in World War II, the original stage and auditorium were dispensed with to make way for a concert hall with a capacity of 1,850 – hence the change of name. The façade, however, is faithful to Schinkel's original design. (Look out for the sculpture of Apollo in his chariot.)

Two cathedrals The twin French and German cathedrals (Französischer Dom, Deutscher Dom) occupy opposite ends of the square. The architect Karl von Gontard, described as an ass by Frederick the Great, lived up to his reputation when one of the complementary cupolas collapsed in 1781. A small museum in the Deutscher Dom charts the history of German democracy from the 19th century to the present with photographs, film and a variety of artefacts. A museum in the Französischer Dom tells the story of the hard-working Huguenots who settled in Berlin in the 17th century, fleeing persecution in France. The Cathedral (minus its baroque tower, a later addition) was built for them. The cathedral's other attractions include the Turmstube restaurant in the tower, and the famous carillon, which plays three times daily.

HIGHLIGHTS

- Konzerthaus
- Statue of Schiller
- Apollo in his chariot
- Deutscher Dom
- Cathedrals' twin towers

Französischer Dom
- Turmstube
- Balustrade view
- Carillon

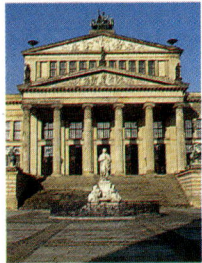

Konzerthaus

INFORMATION

- ✚ J5
- ☎ Französischer Dom: 2291760.
  Deutscher Dom: 22732141
- ◷ Französischer Dom: daily 10–6. Huguenot Museum: Wed–Sat 12–5; Sun 1–5. Deutscher Dom: Tue–Sun 10–5
- Ⓤ U-Bahn Französische Strasse
- 🚌 Bus 147, 257
- Ⓡ Friedrichstrasse
- 🍴 Inexpensive
- ↔ Topography of Terror (➤ 38), Checkpoint Charlie (➤ 40), Unter den Linden (➤ 42)

41

19

UNTER DEN LINDEN

The street 'Under the Lime Trees' – once the heart of imperial Berlin – boasts some fine baroque and neo-classical buildings. The pièce de résistance is Andreas Schlüter's superb sculptures of dying warriors in the courtyard of the Zeughaus.

HIGHLIGHTS

- Deutsche Staatsoper
- Façade of Alte-Königliche Bibliothek
- Statue of Frederick the Great
- Humboldt University
- Neue Wache
- Zeughaus (note especially the masks of dying warriors in the Schlüterhof)
- Cannon (in the Schlüterhof)
- Opernpalais café (details, ➤ 69)
- Hedwigskirche

INFORMATION

- J5
- Unter den Linden 2
- German History Museum (Deutsches Historisches Museum), Zeughaus: 203040. Hedwigskirche: 2034810
- Museum: daily 10–6. Closed Wed
  Hedwigskirche: Mon–Sat 10–5; Sun 12:30–5
- Opernpalais café (£) and restaurant (£££)
- U-Bahn Französische Strasse
- Bus 100, 147, 257
- Friedrichstrasse
- None
- Zeughaus (German History Museum): free
- Gendarmenmarkt (➤ 41), Museums Island (➤ 43), Pergamon Museum (➤ 44), Berlin Cathedral (➤ 45)

Forum Fridericianum The ghost of Frederick the Great presides over the eastern end of Unter den Linden. His equestrian statue, sculpted by Daniel Christian Rauch, stands next to Bebelplatz, once known as the Forum Fridericianum, and intended by the Prussian monarch to hark back to the grandeur of Imperial Rome. Dominating the square is Georg von Knobelsdorff's opera house, the Deutsche Staatsoper. Facing it is the Old Royal Library (Alte-Königliche Bibliothek), completed in 1780 and immediately nicknamed 'the Kommode' (chest of drawers) by quick-witted Berliners. It was here that Nazi propaganda chief Josef Goebbels consigned the works of ideological opponents to the flames in a public book-burning in 1933. Just south of Bebelplatz is the Roman Catholic cathedral, the Hedwigskirche, whose classical lines echo the Pantheon in Rome.

Zeughaus Frederick's civic project was never completed, but the buildings on the opposite side of Unter den Linden keep up imperial appearances. Karl Marx was a student at the Humboldt University, designed by Johann Boumann as a palace for Frederick the Great's brother in 1748. Next comes the Neue Wache (Guardhouse), designed by Schinkel in 1818 to complement Johann Nering's magnificent baroque palace, the Zeughaus (Arsenal) which dates from 1695 and now houses the German History Museum.

MUSEUMS ISLAND

Berlin's renowned collection of antiquities, dispersed during World War II, will by the end of 2000 be reassembled in a complex of museums on an island in the Spree. A visit to Museumsinsel, especially the Pergamon (➤ 44), is an essential part of your stay.

Altes Museum This was the first museum built on the island, in 1830. Karl Schinkel's magnificent classical temple will share with the Pergamon (➤ 44) fabulous collections of sculptures, paintings and artefacts from all corners of the ancient world. The building itself accorded with Schinkel's vision of Berlin as 'Athens on the Spree'. Not content with the overwhelming impression made by the façade, Schinkel has a surprise in store: hidden in the core of the building is a Rotunda inspired by the Pantheon in Rome and lined with statues of the gods.

Neues Museum Berlin's famed Egyptian collections are scheduled to be housed once again in this museum, designed in 1843 by August Stüler. Treasures include the bust of Queen Nefertiti currently in Charlottenburg (➤ 51); it may be that she will be reunited with a similar bust of her husband, King Akhenaten.

Bode-Museum Named after Wilhelm von Bode (1845–1929), for 20 years curator of Museums Island, this 1904 building will exhibit exquisite medieval sculptures (including works by German master Tilman Riemanschneider), early Christian and Byzantine art, and an outstanding coin collection.

Alte Nationalgalerie This gallery will display 19th- and early 20th-century German paintings.

HIGHLIGHTS

● View of Altes Museum from the Lustgarten
● Rotunda of Altes Museum
● *Four Evangelists*, sculpture by Tilman Riemenschneider (Bode-Museum)
● *Unter den Linden*, Franz Krüger (Alte Nationalgalerie)
● *Portrait of Frederick the Great at Potsdam*, Adolph Menzel (Alte Nationalgalerie)
● Papyrus collection (Neues Museum)
● View from Monbijou Bridge

INFORMATION

✚ J5
✉ Museumsinsel
☎ 20905555
🕐 Until the end of 2000 some museums will open only for temporary exhibitions Tue–Sun 10–6
🍴 Café Pergamon ➤ 44
🚇 S-Bahn Hackescher Markt
🚌 Bus 100, 157
🚊 Hackescher Markt
♿ Few
◐ Moderate
↔ Pergamon Museum (➤ 44), Berlin Cathedral (➤ 45)

Schinkel's Rotunda, the Altes Museum

43

21

PERGAMON MUSEUM

HIGHLIGHTS

- 120m frieze on Pergamon Altar
- Market gate from Miletus
- Ishtar Gate
- Façade of Mshatta Palace
- Nebuchadnezzar's throne room
- Figurines from Jericho
- Panelled room from Aleppo
- Bust of the Emperor Caracalla
- Statue of Aphrodite from Myrina
- Mosaic from Hadrian's villa at Tivoli

INFORMATION

- J5
- Am Kupfergraben, Museumsinsel
- 20355500
- Tue–Sun 9–5; large halls also open Mon–Tue
- Café (££)
- S-Bahn Hackescher Markt
- Bus 100, 157
- Hackescher Markt
- Few
- Moderate
- Unter den Linden (➤ 42), Museums Island (➤ 43), Berlin Cathedral (➤ 45)

If you have time to visit only one museum in Berlin, choose the Pergamon. Virtually every corner of the ancient world is represented here.

Like the other museums on Museums Island (Museumsinsel), the Pergamon was built to house the vast haul of antiquities amassed by German archaeologists and adventurers in the 19th century. Recently there has been controversy over the proper home for such antiquities; some people argue that they were wrongfully plundered from ancient sites in the Near East and have no place in Western museums.

Pergamon Altar The most stunning exhibit here is the famous Pergamon Altar from Asia Minor, so huge that it needs a hall 16m high to accommodate it. From Bergama on the west coast of Turkey, it was excavated by Carl Humann in 1878–86. This stupendous monument, dating from about 164 BC, was actually only part of a complex of royal palaces, temples, a library and a theatre. Hardly less impressive is the reconstructed market gateway of Miletus (in western Turkey), built by the Romans in AD 120 during the reign of Emperor Hadrian. The Babylonian Ishtar Gate makes a startling contrast with its brilliantly coloured bricks of glazed clay. Built between 604 and 562 BC, it was dedicated to the goddess of war, Ishtar, whose symbol was a lion.

Antiquities The museum has a splendid collection of Greek and Roman statues (some of which still retain traces of their original vibrant colouring), an exhibition of Islamic art, and displays of figurines, clay tablets and artefacts from Sumeria and other parts of the Middle East.

BERLIN CATHEDRAL

Look no further than Berlin's massive Protestant cathedral for evidence of over-blown imperial pretensions. Intended as a mausoleum for the Hohenzollern dynasty, its vault contains the sarcophagi of more than 90 of them.

Cathedral Architect Julius Raschdorff built the Berliner Dom over the site of a smaller imperial chapel. The existing cathedral was completed in 1905 and opened in the presence of Kaiser Wilhelm II himself. The most impressive feature of the interior is the 74m-high dome, supported by pillars of Silesian sandstone and decorated with mosaics of the Beatitudes by Anton von Werner. In High Renaissance style, it is more than a little reminiscent of St Peter's in Rome. The cathedral was badly bombed during World War II but, after years of neglect, restoration started in 1974 and is now well advanced. Work on the stained-glass windows has been completed.

Lustgarten Just outside the cathedral on Museumsinsel was the pleasure garden which gives the square its name (Lustgarten). The Great Elector is said to have planted potatoes here. Opposite stood the enormous Berliner Schloss, an imposing building dating from the early 18th century and designed by Andreas Schlüter and Johann Eosander von Göethe. The statue of the Great Elector, now in front of Schloss Charlottenburg, once stood here. The Berliner Schloss was destroyed by Allied bombs in World War II but there was recently a campaign to have it rebuilt. The cost, however, will surely be prohibitive.

HIGHLIGHTS

- Lustgarten
- High Renaissance-style façade
- Baptism chapel
- Imperial staircase
- Sarcophagi
- 74m-high dome
- Carved figures above the altar

INFORMATION

- ✚ K5
- ✉ Am Lustgarten
- ☎ 202690
- 🕐 Mon–Sat 9–7; Sun 1–5
- 🍴 None
- Ⓜ U-Bahn Hausvogteiplatz
- 🚌 Bus 100, 157
- 🚉 Hackescher Markt
- ♿ None
- 🎫 Free
- ↔ Unter den Linden (➤ 42), Museums Island (➤ 43), Pergamon Museum (➤ 44)
- ❓ Guided tours in English Thu 3–5:30; Sat 10:30–1:30

The Dom from Marx-Engels-Forum

23

NIKOLAIVIERTEL

HIGHLIGHTS

Nikolaikirche
- Exhibition of Berlin history
- Gothic nave
- *The Good Samaritan*, Michael Ribestein
- Hunger Cloth (in vestry)
- Wooden *Crucifixion* of 1485

Nikolaiviertel
- Ephraimpalais
- Knoblauchhaus
- Zum Nussbaum
- Well outside the pub Zum Paddenwirt

INFORMATION

⊞ K5
✉ Poststrasse
☎ Nikolaikirche: 240020
   Ephraimpalais: 2380900
   Knoblauchhaus: 24313392
🕓 Nikolaikirche: Tue–Sun
   10–6
   Ephraimpalais: Tue–Thu
   9–5; Sat 9–6; Sun 10–5
   Knoblauchhaus:
   Tue–Sun 10–6
🍴 Excellent café (££);
   restaurant (£££)
Ⓤ U-Bahn Klosterstrasse
🚌 Bus 147, 257
🚆 Alexanderplatz
♿ None
♿ Nikolaikirche: moderate
   Ephraimpalais: moderate
   Knoblauchhaus: moderate
↔ Berlin Cathedral (➤ 45),
   Alexanderplatz (➤ 47)

Step back two or three centuries and enjoy a wander through the Nikolai Quarter, a charming pastiche of baroque and neo-classical architecture, with its rows of gabled houses, cobbled streets and quaint shops.

Nikolaikirche The dominating landmark is the twin-spired church which gives the Nikolaiviertel its name. The Nikolaikirche is the oldest church in Berlin, dating originally from 1200 although the present building was not completed until 1470. Seriously damaged in World War II, the beautifully proportioned Gothic nave has been sensitively restored. The church is of great historic importance, for it was here, in 1307, that the two communities of Berlin and Cölln were formally united. The church, now only occasionally used for services, houses a museum of Berlin history that includes models of the medieval city.

Around the Quarter Two other notable buildings recall the lavish lifestyle of Imperial Berlin. The pink stuccoed Knoblauchhaus was designed by Friedrich Wilhelm Dietrichs for one of Berlin's most distinguished families in 1759. Their history is illustrated in a small museum with paintings and Biedermeier furniture. The extravagant Ephraimpalais in rococo style, with attractive golden balconies and stone cherubs, once belonged to Frederick the Great's banker, Nathan Ephraim. The interior is decorated with art of the 17th to the 19th centuries.

Probably the most picturesque streets are Eiergasse and the one named after its cheery reconstruction of a famous 16th-century Berlin inn, Zum Nussbaum ('At the Nut Tree') – a good refreshment stop if it isn't too crowded.

ALEXANDERPLATZ

A victim of East German town planning, 'Alex' (as the square is affectionately known to Berliners) is waiting to be revamped by a new generation of architects with a brief to return this historic old market place to the people.

Historic square Alexanderplatz was colonised by Berlin's burgeoning working class in the middle of the 19th century. Crime flourished here too, so it is no accident that the police headquarters was located within striking distance. Today Alexanderplatz is a bleak open space crying out for rebuilding and development.

TV tower The Fernsehturm rises like an unlovely flower from the centre of the square. Its single virtue is its great height, at 362m exceeding even Paris's Eiffel Tower. Climb it on a fine day for panoramic views of the city. Hans Kolhoff's ambitious plans for the future development of the square below may never be realised owing to the prohibitive cost.

Other attractions Two historic buildings add lustre to the fringes of Alexanderplatz. City Hall was formerly known as the Red Town Hall (Rotes Rathaus) from its colour. The architect, Heinrich Friedrich Waesemann, was inspired by the municipal architecture of Renaissance Italy when he designed the building in 1869. The Marienkirche, Berlin's second oldest church, is a survivor from an earlier age. The nave is 15th-century, the lantern tower a flight of fancy added by Karl Gotthard Langhans in 1790. A plague epidemic in 1484 is commemorated in *Dance of Death* (*Totentanz*) a large medieval wall-painting.

HIGHLIGHTS

- Fernsehturm
- City Hall
- World Time Clock
- Neptune Fountain
- Forum Hotel
- Marx-Engels statue
- Kaufhof department store (➤ 70)
- Marienkirche
- *Dance of Death* (*Totentanz*) frieze

Fernsehturm and City Hall

INFORMATION

- ✚ K5
- 🕐 Fernsehturm: daily 9AM–11:30PM (2nd and 4th Tue of each month 1PM–11:30PM) Marienkirche: Mon–Thu 10–noon, 1–5; Sat noon–4:30
- 🍴 Cafés (£); Fernsehturm restaurant with view (£££)
- 🚇 S- or U-Bahn Alexanderplatz
- 🚌 Bus 100, 157, 257
- ♿ Fernsehturm: moderate
- ↔ Nikolaiviertel (➤ 46)

47

25

Schloss Köpenick

Standing in peaceful parkland on the Schlossinsel, an island formed by the rivers Dahme and Spree, this time-worn 17th-century former residence of the rulers of the Mark Brandenburg has its own off-beat charm.

HIGHLIGHTS

- Dutch baroque façade
- Stucco ceiling of the Wappensaal
- Collection of gold and silver tableware
- Swiss panelled room
- Jugendstil glass
- Aubert Parent's carved reliefs
- 18th-century furniture
- Baroque chapel
- Schlossinsel
- View of the old fishing port of Kietz

INFORMATION

- ✚ Off map to southeast
- ✉ Schlossinsel
- ☎ 6572651
- ◷ Tue–Sun 9–5
- 🍴 Café (£)
- Ⓢ S-Bahn Köpenick
- 🚌 Bus 167, 360
- 🚣 Köpenick
- ♿ None
- ✋ Inexpensive

The Dutch baroque façade

Royal residence The current Schloss, built in the Dutch baroque style by Rutger van Langefelt for Elector Friedrich in 1681, stands on the site of a 9th-century Slav fortress. Its most remarkable feature is the Hall of Arms (Wappensaal), with a stuccoed ceiling by the Italian, Giovanni Carove. Classical figures support the coats of arms, principally of the Mark Brandenburg. The chapel (not always open) is a distinguished example of Arnold Nering's work, dating from 1682–5.

Museum The Schloss also houses a branch of the Museum of Applied Art (Kunstgewerbemuseum). The display includes silverware rescued from the ruins of the Berlin Royal Palace at the end of World War II. There is furniture by David Roentgens, including an elegant cabinet dating from 1779; a small but highly prized collection of glassware; and a dinner service belonging to Frederick II, manufactured by the famous Royal Porcelain Factory.

Köpenick Köpenick was a hotbed of working-class resistance to the Nazis: more than 90 people perished in Blutwoche, the 'week of blood', in 1933. Many others were imprisoned and tortured. The events are commemorated by a memorial in Puchanstrasse. Today the old town (Altstadt) is undergoing extensive restoration. Its dilapidated but picturesque streets, dating from the 13th century, retain an antique flavour and are worth exploring.

BERLIN's *best*

Museums	50–51	Political Sights	55
Galleries	52	Parks & Gardens	56
Places of Worship	53	Views	57
Bridges	54	Statues & Monuments	58
		Attractions for Children	59
		Free Attractions	60

MUSEUMS

City of museums

Berlin's museums are justifiably renowned the world over for their comprehensiveness, diversity and sheer abundance. Many subjects have two collections devoted to them – a situation which arose in the confusion of the divided city after World War II, when many of the artefacts were stolen or dispersed and had to be collected together again. The fantastic archaeological finds of the 19th century, brought here by the cartload, make the museums specialising in antiquities a treat to savour.

Bust of Nefertiti, Egyptian Museum (due to move to Museums Island in 2000)

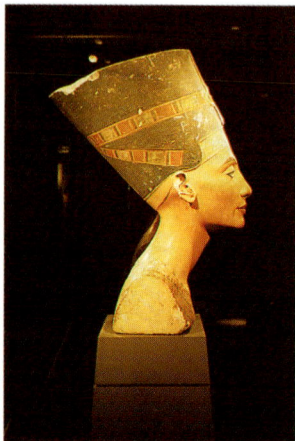

See Top 25 Sights for
CHECKPOINT CHARLIE MUSEUM (HAUS AM CHECKPOINT CHARLIE) ➤ 40
ETHNOGRAPHICAL MUSEUM (MUSEUM FÜR VÖLKERKUNDE), DAHLEM ➤ 30
GERMAN HISTORY MUSEUM (DEUTSCHES HISTORISCHES MUSEUM), ZEUGHAUS ➤ 42
HISTORICAL EXHIBITION IN DEUTSCHER DOM ➤ 41
HUGUENOT MUSEUM (HUGENOTTENMUSEUM), IN FRANZÖSISCHER DOM ➤ 41
MUSEUM OF APPLIED ART (KUNSTGEWERBEMUSEUM), KULTURFORUM ➤ 36
MUSEUM OF MUSICAL INSTRUMENTS (MUSIKINSTRUMENTEN-MUSEUM), KULTURFORUM ➤ 35
PERGAMON MUSEUM ➤ 44

ALLIED FORCES MUSEUM (ALLIIERTEN-MUSEUM)

The former US mission plays host to this exhibition on the Allied occupation of Berlin.

Off map to the south · Clayallee 135 · 8181990 · Tue–Sun 10–6 · U-Bahn Oskar-Helene-Heim · Free

BERLIN MUSEUM

When the city's excellent history museum reopens (during 1999) it will include a permanent exhibition on Jewish life.

J7 · Lindenstrasse 61 · 23809030 · Closed for restoration until 1999

BRECHT'S HOUSE (BRECHT-HAUS)

The famous German playwright Bertolt Brecht (1898–1956) lived in this house for the last three years of his life. Archive material on Brecht is kept here.

H4 · Chausseestrasse 125 · 2829916 · Tue–Fri 10–12; Thu 5–7; Sat 9:30–12 and 12:30–2 · U-Bahn Oranienburger Tor · Moderate; guided tour only

BRÖHAN MUSEUM

In 1983 Professor Karl Bröhan presented his superb collection of Jugendstil and art-deco crafts to the city. The highlight of the museum is a series of rooms decorated in the styles of the leading designers of the period.

B5 · Schlossstrasse 1a · 3214029 · Tue–Sun 10–6 · Bus 109, 110, 145 · Moderate

German Technical Museum

EGYPTIAN MUSEUM (ÄGYPTISCHES MUSEUM)

The undisputed star of this rich collection (due to move in 2000 to Museums Island (► 43) is the bust of Tutankhamun's aunt, Queen Nefertiti, dating from about 1340 BC. There are also mummies, death masks, jewellery and even games.

➕ C5 ✉ Schlossstrasse 70 ☎ 32091261 🕐 Tue–Fri 10–6; Sat–Sun 11–6 🚌 Bus 109, 110, 145 💷 Moderate

GERMAN TECHNICAL MUSEUM (MUSEUM FÜR VERKEHR UND TECHNIK)

A thoroughly entertaining and beautifully presented exhibition in the locomotive sheds of the old Anhalter train station. Everything from biplanes and vintage cars to model ships and computers.

➕ H7 ✉ Trebbiner Strasse 9 ☎ 254840 🕐 Tue–Fri 9–5:30; Sat–Sun 10–6 🚇 U-Bahn Gleisdreieck 💷 Moderate

MUSEUM OF BERLIN WORKING-CLASS LIFE

Reconstructed rooms in one of the notorious Mietskasernen (tenement blocks) colourfully reveal life as lived by workers at the start of the 20th century.

➕ L3 ✉ Husemannstrasse 12 ☎ 4422514 🕐 Mon–Thu 10–3 🚇 U-Bahn Eberswalder Strasse 💷 Inexpensive

MUSEUMS OF INDIAN AND EAST ASIAN ART (MUSEUM FÜR INDISCHE KUNST; OSTASIATISCHE KUNST)

Two museums within a complex of galleries in Dahlem, presenting the art and culture of India and the Far East with style and imagination.

➕ Off map to south ✉ Laristrasse 8 ☎ 8301399 🕐 Tue–Fri 10–6; Sat–Sun 11–6 🚇 U-Bahn Dahlem-Dorf 💷 Moderate

NEW SYNAGOGUE (NEUE SYNAGOGE)

Visible from all over the Mitte on account of its golden dome, this historic building dates from 1866 and is now a centre for Jewish studies. Inside is a moving exhibition on the history of the community.

➕ J4 ✉ Oranienburger Strasse 28–30 ☎ No phone 🕐 Sun–Thu 10–6 🚇 S-Bahn Oranienburger Strasse 💷 Inexpensive

POTSDAM FILM MUSEUM

Located near the famous Babelsberg Studios, where Marlene Dietrich was one of the stars. Fascinating exhibition on the history of the German film industry.

➕ Off map to southwest ✉ Breite Strasse, Potsdam ☎ (0331) 293675 🕐 Daily noon–midnight 🚇 S-Bahn Potsdam Stadt 💷 Moderate

Troy's treasures

Rumours abound concerning the return of Berlin's most famous archaeological treasure, the 10,000 objects recovered by Heinrich Schliemann from the site of what he assumed to be the ancient city of Troy in the 1870s. Rather fancifully, as it turned out, Schliemann attributed the vast hoard of gold to the Homeric hero King Priam himself. The collection disappeared during World War II, but has recently been on show in Moscow.

GALLERIES

Die Brücke

Anyone wishing for an introduction to 20th-century art could hardly do better than visit the Brücke Museum on the edge of the Grunewald forest. The artistic movement known as Die Brücke (the Bridge), which flourished between 1905 and 1913, was in the vanguard of German Expressionism. The landscapes and portraits by Ludwig Kirchner, Karl Schmidt-Rottluff, Emil Nolde, Max Pechstein and others bridge the gap between figurative and abstract art and make Cubism more comprehensible.

See Top 25 Sights for
BAUHAUS MUSEUM (BAUHAUS-ARCHIV) ➤ 34
EPHRAIMPALAIS ➤ 46
GALLERY OF ROMANTIC PAINTING (GALERIE DER ROMANTIK), CHARLOTTENBURG ➤ 31
KÄTHE KOLLWITZ MUSEUM ➤ 32
MUSEUMS ISLAND (MUSEUMSINSEL) ➤ 43
NEW NATIONAL GALLERY (NEUE NATIONALGALERIE), KULTURFORUM ➤ 35
PICTURE GALLERY (GEMÄLDEGALERIE), KULTURFORUM ➤ 35

BERGGRUEN COLLECTION

A hugely stimulating exhibition of paintings and sculptures by Picasso and his contemporaries. There are nearly 70 pieces by Picasso, as well as works by Klee, Braque, Giacometti and Cézanne.
✚ B5 ✉ Schlossstrasse 1 ☎ 20905555 🕐 Tue–Fri 10–6; Sat–Sun 11–6 🚌 Bus 109, 110, 145 💷 Moderate

BRÜCKE MUSEUM

This small, modern gallery exhibits work from the group of 20th-century German artists known as Die Brücke (see panel).
✚ Off map to south ✉ Bussardsteig 9 ☎ 8312029 🕐 Wed–Mon 11–5 🚌 Bus 115 💷 Moderate

Martin-Gropius-Bau

EASTSIDE GALLERY

Graffiti art as revealed on a 1.3km section of the former Berlin Wall. Said to be the world's largest open-air art gallery.
✚ M6 ✉ Mühlenstrasse 🚇 U-Bahn Schlesisches Tor 💷 Free

KUPFERSTICH-KABINETT

Literally 'engravings room', this is a collection of drawings and prints by some of the great European artists, including Cranach, Dürer, Pieter Bruegel the Elder, Rembrandt and Kandinsky.
✚ G6 ✉ Matthäikirchplatz 8 ☎ 2666 🕐 Tue–Fri 9–5 🚇 U- or S-Bahn Potsdamer Platz 💷 Moderate

MARTIN-GROPIUS-BAU

Designed by architect Martin Gropius in the style of the Italian Renaissance, and an interesting building in itself, this is a venue for major art exhibitions.
✚ H6 ✉ Stresemannstrasse 110 ☎ 254860 🕐 Tue–Sun 10–8 🚇 U-Bahn Potsdamer Platz 💷 Moderate

PLACES OF WORSHIP

See Top 25 Sights for
BERLIN CATHEDRAL (BERLINER DOM) ➤ 45
**FRENCH CATHEDRAL
    (FRANZÖSISCHER DOM)** ➤ 41
HEDWIGSKIRCHE ➤ 42
**KAISER WILHELM MEMORIAL CHURCH (KAISER
    WILHELM GEDÄCHTNISKIRCHE)** ➤ 33
MARIENKIRCHE ➤ 47
NIKOLAIKIRCHE ➤ 46

FRIEDRICHWERDERSCHE KIRCHE

Berlin's celebrated architect Karl Friedrich Schinkel designed this church in neo-Gothic style in 1824. It is now a museum honouring his work.

✚ J5 ✉ Werderstrasse ☎ 2081323 🕐 Tue–Sun 10–6
🚇 U-Bahn Hausvogteiplatz ♿ Moderate

K F Schinkel

No man left more of an impression on the architecture of Berlin than Karl Friedrich Schinkel (1781–1840). Mostly he favoured the classical style, as in the Konzerthaus (formerly the Schauspielhaus) and the Neue Wache. But in designing the Friedrichwerdersche Kirche he turned for inspiration to medieval Gothic. The beautifully proportioned nave is the setting for a satisfying exhibition on his life's work.

*Inside Friedrich-
werdersche Kirche*

GETHSEMANE KIRCHE

This church shot to overnight fame in 1989 when it became the spiritual centre of the resistance movement to the East German Communist regime. Nightly peace vigils drew the world's media.

✚ L2 ✉ Stargarder Strasse ☎ 442850 🕐 For services
🚇 U- or S-Bahn Schönhauser Allee

NEW SYNAGOGUE (NEUE SYNAGOGUE)

The stunning dome of this building is one of Berlin's landmarks. Designed by Eduard Knoblauch and August Stüler, it survived the infamous Reichskristallnacht, on 9 November 1938, when the Nazis destroyed Jewish buildings.

✚ J4 ✉ Oranienburger Strasse 28–30 ☎ Foundation (Stiftung)
2801253 🚇 S-Bahn Oranienburger Strasse

SOPHIENKIRCHE

Berlin's sole surviving baroque church, designed by J. F. Grael, was completed in 1734 but is now in need of restoration.

✚ K4 ✉ Grosse Hamburger Strasse 🚇 U-Bahn Weinmeisterstrasse

BRIDGES

Rosa Luxemburg

The most dramatic event to occur at one of Berlin's many bridges was the recovery of the body of communist agitator Rosa Luxemburg in January 1919. After her murder by right-wing army officers in the Tiergarten, her corpse was dumped into the Landwehrkanal. It was found weeks later under the Lichtensteinbrücke.

Moltkebrücke

See Top 25 Sights for GLIENICKER BRÜCKE ➤ 26

FRIEDRICHS-BRÜCKE
This elegant bridge, built in 1892, provides a fine view of the Berliner Dom.
➕ K5   ✉ Bodestrasse   🚇 S-Bahn Hackescher Markt

GERTRAUDENBRÜCKE
Gertraud was a favourite saint of the fisher folk who used to ply the waters here in the Middle Ages. Bronze water rats decorate the base of her statue.
➕ K6   ✉ Gertraudenstrasse   🚇 U-Bahn Spittelmarkt

JUNGFERNBRÜCKE
This drawbridge, dating from 1798, was once the haunt of Huguenot working girls selling silk and lace.
➕ K5   ✉ Friedrichsgracht   🚇 U-Bahn Spittelmarkt

LESSINGBRÜCKE
Lessing (1729–81) is one of Germany's best-known playwrights. The sandstone piers of 'his' bridge are decorated with scenes from his dramas.
➕ F4   ✉ Lessingstrasse   🚇 U-Bahn Turmstrasse

MOABITER BRÜCKE
This bridge of 1864 is famous for the four bears that decorate it (the bear being the symbol of Berlin).
➕ F5   ✉ Bellevue Ufer   🚇 S-Bahn Bellevue

MOLTKEBRÜCKE
Named after a hero of the Franco-Prussian war, this belligerent bridge is guarded by Prussian eagles and cherubs wielding swords, spears, trumpets and drums. It was completed in 1891.
➕ G5   ✉ Moltkestrasse   🚇 S-Bahn Lehrter Stadtbahnhof

OBERBAUMBRÜCKE
More than 500 different kinds of tiles were used in the renovation of what was once Berlin's longest bridge.
➕ N7   ✉ Mühlenstrasse   🚇 U-Bahn Schlesisches Tor

SCHLEUSENBRÜCKE
This simple iron bridge is decorated with historic scenes of Berlin.
➕ K5   ✉ Werderstrasse   🚇 U-Bahn Hausvogteiplatz

SCHLOSSBRÜCKE
Karl Friedrich Schinkel designed a new bridge to replace the decrepit Hundebrücke in 1819. Named after a royal palace which no longer exists, it is decorated by a series of statues of Greek gods.
➕ K5   ✉ Unter den Linden   🚇 U-Bahn Hausvogteiplatz

POLITICAL SIGHTS

See Top 25 Sights for
**BRANDENBURG GATE
(BRANDENBURGER TOR) ➤ 39
CHECKPOINT CHARLIE ➤ 40
SACHSENHAUSEN CONCENTRATION
CAMP ➤ 29
TOPOGRAPHY OF TERROR
(TOPOGRAPHIE DES TERRORS) ➤ 38**

MEMORIAL TO GERMAN RESISTANCE (GEDENKSTÄTTE DEUTSCHER WIDERSTAND)

Known as the Bendlerblock, this annexe to the Admiralty became the focus of von Stauffenberg's ill-fated conspiracy against Hitler on 20 July 1944. It now houses an exhibition on opposition to Hitler.

🔲 G6 ✉ Stauffenbergstrasse 13 ☎ 26542202 🕐 Mon–Fri 9–6; Sat–Sun 9–1 🚇 U-Bahn Kurfürstrasse 🎟 Free

PLÖTZENSEE MEMORIAL (GEDENKSTÄTTE PLÖTZENSEE)

More than 2,500 people were executed in this infamous Nazi prison. Today an exhibition and memorial commemorate the victims.

🔲 D2 ✉ Hüttigpfad ☎ 3443226 🕐 Daily 8:30–6 🚈 S-Bahn Tiergarten 🚌 Bus 123 🎟 Free

REICHSTAG

The German parliament building of 1884 is due to re-open in 1999. It will accommodate the parliament of the German Republic.

🔲 H5 ✉ Platz der Republik ☎ 39770 🚈 S-Bahn Unter den Linden

SCHÖNEBERG TOWN HALL (RATHAUS SCHÖNEBERG)

From 1948 to 1989 this was the municipal headquarters of West Berlin. President Kennedy made his famous 'Ich bin ein Berliner' speech from the balcony in June 1963.

🔲 F9 ✉ Martin-Luther-Strasse 🚈 U-Bahn Rathaus Schöneberg 🎟 Free

WANNSEE CONFERENCE CENTRE (GEDENKSTÄTTE HAUS DER WANNSEE KONFERENZ)

In this innocuous-looking mansion on the shores of Lake Wannsee, leading Nazis plotted the mass extermination of Europe's 11 million Jews. The exhibition tells the whole horrific story.

🔲 Off map to southwest ✉ Am Grossen Wannsee 58 ☎ 8050010 🕐 Tue–Fri 10–6; Sat–Sun 2–6 🚈 S-Bahn Wannsee 🚌 Bus 114 🎟 Free

The Reichstag

Once at the cutting edge of the Cold War (the Berlin Wall ran directly behind the building), the Reichstag has had a troubled but colourful history. In February 1933 the Nazis stage-managed a fire in the building as an excuse to do away with the democratic institutions of the Weimar Republic. The new design preserves the shell of the building but the interior has been gutted to create a new parliamentary chamber.

The Reichstag

PARKS & GARDENS

See Top 25 Sights for
TIERGARTEN ➤ 37

BOTANICAL GARDEN (BOTANISCHER GARTEN)
More than 18,000 varieties of plants and flowers in beautifully landscaped grounds.

➕ Off map to south ✉ Königin-Luise-Strasse 6–8
☎ 830060 🕐 Tue–Sun 10–5
🚇 U-Bahn Rathaus Steglitz ♿ Moderate

BRITZER GARTEN
Created for the National Garden Show in 1985, the 100-hectare site is a favourite with cyclists, dog-owners and families. There is a lake, nature trails and a restaurant.

➕ Off map to south ✉ Sangerhauser Weg 1
☎ 7009060 🕐 Summer, daily 9–8; winter, daily 9–4
🚌 Bus 144, 179, 181 ♿ Free

FREIZEITPARK TEGEL
Possibly the best Berlin park – certainly for children – with everything laid on including table tennis, trampolines, volleyball, rowing, paddle-boats and even chess. Pleasure cruisers depart from the Greenwich promenade near by.

➕ Off map to northwest ✉ An der Malche 🚇 U-Bahn Alt-Tegel

TIERPARK BERLIN-FRIEDRICHSFELDE
Berlin's second zoo is situated on the eastern side of the city in grounds that once formed part of Schloss Friedrichsfelde. Concerts and other events are held regularly in the restored palace.

➕ Off map to east ✉ Am Tierpark 125 ☎ 515310 🕐 Daily 9–dark 🚇 U-Bahn Tierpark

TREPTOWER PARK
The largest green space on the eastern side of the city spreads out along the banks of the Spree. Fairs and other entertainments are often held here.

➕ N8 ✉ Puschkinallee 🚇 S-Bahn Treptower Park

VIKTORIAPARK
Best known for Karl Friedrich Schinkel's Monument to the Wars of Liberation (1813–15), approached from a row of terraces and gardens, from the summit of which are views of Berlin. Children's playground.

➕ H8 ✉ Kreuzbergstrasse 🚇 U-Bahn Platz der Luftbrücke

VOLKSPARK JUNGFERNHEIDE
This park on the northern fringe of Charlottenburg offers open-air swimming, boat hire, hiking, sports fields and a theatre.

➕ B2 ✉ Saatwinkler Damm 🚇 U-Bahn Siemensdamm

The Botanical Garden

Green Berlin

Flying over Berlin, every visitor is struck by the forest and lakes that surround the city, from Wannsee and the Grunewald in the west to Müggelsee and the Spreewald in the east. The city itself is unusually well provided with municipal parks – on hot Sunday afternoons they are the Berliners' favourite venue for barbecues, picnics and walking the dog.

VIEWS

See Top 25 Sights for
FERNSEHTURM ► 47
FRENCH CATHEDRAL
    (FRANZÖSISCHER DOM) ► 41
GRUNEWALDTURM ► 28
JULIUSTURM, SPANDAU ► 27
SIEGESSÄULE ► 37

BLOCKHAUS NIKOLSKOE ► 62, 63

EUROPA-CENTER ► 77

BELL-TOWER (GLOCKENTURM) OF OLYMPIC STADIUM (OLYMPIASTADION)

The 77m-high bell-tower affords excellent views of the Waldbühne (an open-air stadium used for rock concerts), the Grunewald and the Havel.

🔳 Off map to west 🖂 Olympisches Tor ☎ 3058123
🕓 Apr–Oct daily 9:30–5:30 🚇 U-Bahn Olympiastadion (Ost)
💶 Inexpensive

FUNKTURM

Berlin's broadcasting tower was built in 1924–6 to a design by Heinrich Straumer (see panel).

🔳 A6 🖂 Messedamm ☎ Restaurant: 30382996 🕓 Tower: daily 10–8. Restaurant: daily 11–11 🚇 U-Bahn Kaiserdamm
💶 Moderate

'MONT KLAMOTT'

Otherwise known as Grosser Bunkerberg, this is one of the artificial mounds created from rubble cleared from Berlin after World War II. Views of Prenzlauer Berg and points east.

🔳 M4 🖂 Friedenstrasse 🚇 U-Bahn Strausberger Platz

MÜGGELTURM

A 30m-high tower by the Teufelsee with views of the lake and forest scenery of the Müggelsee. (No lift.)

🔳 Off map to southeast 🖂 Kleiner Müggelberg ☎ 6569812
🕓 Daily 8–dusk 🚌 Bus 169
💶 Inexpensive

PARK BABELSBERG

Wonderful views across the Havel towards Potsdam and the Glienicker Bridge from the grounds of this neo-Gothic Schloss built by Schinkel in 1833.

🔳 Off map to southwest
🖂 Allee nach Glienicke
🚌 Bus 691 💶 Free

The Funkturm

A symbol of German technical advance when it was first erected, Berlin's broadcasting tower bears a faint resemblance to the Eiffel Tower in Paris and was nicknamed the Langer Lulatsch (Bean Pole) by city wits. The restaurant is at a mere 55m, so if you are dining, first take the lift to the 126m-high viewing platform which overlooks the Grunewald forest in one direction and western Berlin in the other.

The Olympic Stadium

STATUES & MONUMENTS

See Top 25 Sights for
SIEGESSÄULE ➤ 37
STATUE OF FREDERICK THE GREAT ➤ 42

Marx and Engels

Unlike the statue of Lenin at Platz der Vereinten Nationen, the monolithic bronze sculptures of Karl Marx and Friedrich Engels will probably survive if only because of their sheer bulk. Just after the Wall came down a sharp-witted East Berliner spray-painted the plinth with an apology on their behalf: 'We're sorry, it's not our fault – maybe next time things will turn out better.'

HENRY MOORE SCULPTURE, HAUS DER KULTUREN DER WELT

The British artist Henry Moore designed several statues for Berlin. This one, *Large Butterfly*, 'flutters' over a shallow lake outside the Kongresshalle.

➕ G5 ✉ John-Foster-Dulles-Allee 🚇 S-Bahn Unter den Linden

KLEIST'S GRAVE (KLEISTGRAB)

In a secluded spot in Wannsee is the grave of the Romantic poet Heinrich von Kleist, who committed suicide here with his mistress in 1811.

➕ Off map to southwest ✉ Bismarckstrasse 🚇 S-Bahn Wannsee

MARX AND ENGELS

The two founders of Communism stand forlorn in a tawdry garden near Alexanderplatz (see panel).

➕ K5 ✉ Rathausstrasse 🚇 U-Bahn Alexanderplatz

MATSCHINSKY-DENNINGHOF SCULPTURE

To mark the 750th Anniversary of the founding of Berlin, Matschinsky and Denninghof contrived a sculpture that was intended to symbolise the schizophrenic existence of what was then still a divided city.

➕ F7 ✉ Tauentzienstrasse 🚇 U-Bahn Wittenbergplatz

MONUMENT TO THE WARS OF LIBERATION ➤ 56

Statues of Marx and Engels

SCHLOSSBRÜCKE ➤ 54

SOVIET WAR MEMORIAL (SOWJETISCHES EHRENMAL)

Architecturally speaking, a heavy-handed commemoration of the 20,000 soldiers of the Red Army who died liberating Berlin.

➕ H5 ✉ Strasse des 17 Juni 🚇 S-Bahn Unter den Linden

ZILLE

Known affectionately to Berliners as 'The Poker', the statue to Heinrich Zille (1858–1929), commemorates the artist famed for his satirical contributions to the magazine *Simplizissimus*.

➕ L6 ✉ Am Köllnischen Park 🚇 U-Bahn Märkisches Museum

ATTRACTIONS FOR CHILDREN

BABELSBERG FILM STUDIO
Occupying the site of the old Ufa studios where
Marlene Dietrich began her career, this new theme
park takes a behind-the-scenes look at how films are
made. The 5–6-hour tour covers movie stunts,
special effects, pyrotechnics, action scenes, make-
up, and more.

⊞ Off map   ✉ Grossbeerenstrasse, Babelsberg   ☎ 0331 7212750
🕐 Daily 10–6   🚇 S-Bahn Babelsberg   💷 Expensive

FREIZEITPARK TEGEL ➤ 56

GRIPS-THEATER
The show is in German, but language barriers are not
a problem with these puppets.

⊞ F5   ✉ Altonaer Strasse 22   ☎ 3914004   🕐 Mon–Fri noon–6;
Sat–Sun 12–5   🚇 U-Bahn Hansaplatz   💷 Expensive

MONBIJOU PARK
Conveniently situated near Museums Island,
the park has a playground and paddling pool for
toddlers.

⊞ J4   ✉ Oranienburger Strasse   🚇 S-Bahn Hackescher Markt

PEACOCK ISLAND (PFAUENINSEL)
Not only peacocks, but a model farm and nature and
bird reserve in a picturesque Wannsee setting.

⊞ Off map to southwest   ✉ Nikolskoer Weg   ☎ 8053042
🕐 Ferry daily 8–8   🚌 216   💷 Inexpensive

ZEISS-GROSSPLANETARIUM
Berlin has three planetariums and observatories. This
one gives special monthly shows for children.

⊞ M2   ✉ Prenzlauer Allee 80   ☎ 4218450   🕐 Telephone for
show times   🚇 S-Bahn Prenzlauer Allee   💷 Moderate

Transport and Technology

The German Technical Museum
(➤ 51) is possibly the most child-
orientated museum in Berlin. Its
greatest attraction is that most of
the displays are hands-on and
there is even an experiment room
where children can play with
computers and other gadgets. The
transport section covers
everything from ox-carts to
vintage cars while technology
embraces printing presses, looms,
street organs and much else
besides.

*A shoal on the wall
outside the zoo, in
Budapester Strasse*

ZOO AND AQUARIUM (ZOOLOGISCHER GARTEN)
This is the more conveniently located of Berlin's two
zoos.

⊞ F6   ✉ Budapester Strasse   🕐 Summer: daily 9–6:30; winter:
daily 9–5   🚇 U- or S-Bahn Zoologischer Garten   💷 Expensive

FREE ATTRACTIONS

See Top 25 Sights for
BATHING IN GRUNEWALD ➤ 28
GERMAN HISTORY MUSEUM
   (DEUTSCHES HISTORISCHES MUSEUM) ➤ 42
LISTENING TO BUSKERS ON
   BREITSCHEIDPLATZ ➤ 33
KAISER WILHELM MEMORIALCHURCH ➤ 33
ORGAN RECITALS IN BERLIN CATHEDRAL ➤ 45
SACHSENHAUSEN
   CONCENTRATION CAMP ➤ 29
TIERGARTEN AND OTHER PARKS ➤ 37, 56

Moneysavers

As in most large cities, the best free entertainment in Berlin usually comes from wandering the streets and observing everyday life. Otherwise most attractions in the city make a charge, but this is usually quite reasonable and there are reductions for children, students and senior citizens. Some museums offer free admission on Sundays and public holidays. Also free are the various memorial museums, for example the Memorial to German Resistance (➤ 55) and the Plötzensee Memorial (➤ 55).

ART GALLERIES
Many of the commercial art galleries (➤ 73) are free.

BIKE RENTAL
Well, *almost* free…Biking is the cheapest way of getting about the city quickly and pleasurably. Bikes can be rented from:
Fahrrad International ➕ D8 ✉ Uhlandstrasse 106A
☎ 8615237 🚇 U Bahn Hohenzollernplatz
Fahrrad Freese ➕ L2 ✉ Prenzlauer Allee 216
☎ 4407078 🚇 S-Bahn Prenzlauer Allee
Bahrdt im Zentrum ➕ D6 ✉ Kantstrasse 88–9
☎ 3238129 🚇 S-Bahn Savignyplatz

INTERIOR OF WITTENBERGPLATZ U-BAHN STATION
The splendid 1920s art-deco booking hall has wooden ticket offices, original tiling and colourful period posters advertising the likes of Opel cars and Bechstein grand pianos.
➕ F7 ✉ Tauentzienstrasse
🚇 U-Bahn Wittenbergplatz

WANNSEE–KLADOW FERRY
The enjoyable ferry ride from Wannsee to Kladow is inexpensive (free if you have an Umweltkarte transport card ➤ 90).
➕ Off map to southwest
✉ Wannsee Pier 🚌 BVG Line F10

The Tiergarten, free and right in the middle of Berlin

WATCHING BUILDING DEVELOPMENTS
The Berlin authorities are so conscious of the transformation of their city that building sites such as Potsdamer Platz often come complete with viewing platforms and information offices.
➕ H6 ✉ Potsdamer Platz ☎ 2266240 🕐 Information box
Mon–Sat 9–7 (Thu 9–9) 🚇 U- or S-Bahn Potsdamer Platz

BERLIN
where to...

EAT — 62–69

German Restaurants — 62–63

International Restaurants 64–65

Asian & Vegetarian
  Restaurants — 66

Middle Eastern, Turkish &
  Out-of-Town Restaurants — 67

Cafés — 68–69

SHOP — 70–77

Department Stores &
  Souvvenirs — 70

Boutiques & Designer Clothes — 71

Secondhand & Offbeat — 72

Galleries — 73

Antiques, Glass & Porcelain — 74

Markets & Foodshops — 75

The Best of the Rest — 76–77

BE ENTERTAINED — 78–83

Theatres & Concerts — 78

Cabaret — 79

Pubs, Bars& Clubs — 80–81

Folk, Jazz & Rock — 82

Sport — 83

STAY — 84–86

Luxury Hotels — 84

Mid-Range Hotels — 85

Budget Accommodation — 86

GERMAN RESTAURANTS

Prices

The restaurants in this section are in three categories shown by £ signs. Expect to pay per person for a meal, excluding drink

£   up to DM25

££   up to DM50

£££   over DM50

German fare

Traditional German food is not for the faint-hearted. Plates come piled high with the two staples, meat (usually pork) and potatoes, often accompanied by pickled cabbage (Sauerkraut), peas or the ubiquitous gherkin. Meatballs (Bouletten) and savoury potato pancakes (Kartoffelpuffer) are Berlin specialities. Young Germans with a more delicate palate are rebelling against this high-calorie diet in favour of the New German cuisine offered by an increasing number of restaurants – Funkturm is a typical example.

ALTES LUXEMBURG (£££)
One of the best restaurants in the city. Karl Wannemacher has a way with herbs.

C6   Windscheidstrasse 31   3238730   Tue–Sat 7PM–11PM   U-Bahn Sophie-Charlotten-Platz

ALTES ZOLLHAUS (£££)
An attractive half-timbered former customs house on the Landwehrkanal. New German cuisine; fine wines.

K7   Carl-Herz-Ufer 30   6923300   Tue–Sat 6–11   U-Bahn Prinzenstrasse

AM JULIUSTURM (£££)
Eat well (if not cheaply) in the tower of a Renaissance fortress. A medieval banqueting experience.

Off map to west   Juliusturm, Spandau Zitadelle   3342106   Tue–Fri 6PM–midnight; Sat–Sun 11AM–midnight   U-Bahn Zitadelle

BERLINER STUBE (££)
A large restaurant with terrace, specialising in Berlin cooking, including Eisbein and Berliner leber (liver).

E7   Los Angeles Platz 1   2127750   Daily noon–midnight   U-Bahn Kurfürstendamm

BLOCKHAUS NIKOLSKOE (£££)
The views are superb, but this is an open secret with Berliners (► 63 panel).

Off map to southwest   Nikolskoer Weg   8052914   Fri–Wed 10AM–midnight   S-Bahn Wannsee then bus 216

ERMELERHAUS (££)
An 18th-century house with a rococo interior. If the Weinrestaurant is beyond your budget, try the homely atmosphere and honest German fare in the cellar – Raabe Dile.

K6   Mörkisches Ufer 10–12   240620   Daily noon–11PM   U-Bahn Markisches Museum

FORSTHAUS PAULSBORN (£££)
This stately residence in the Grunewald forest offers coffee, cakes, ice cream and a full traditional German menu.

Off map to southwest   Am Grunewaldsee   8138010   Tue–Sun 11AM–midnight   U-Bahn Oskar-Helene-Heim then bus 115

FUNKTURM (£££)
Updated German cuisine from a vantage point of the radio tower, 55m above Berlin.

A6   Messedamm 22   30383999   Daily 11:30AM–11PM   S-Bahn Witzleben

GASTHAUS BUNDSCHUH (££)
Kreuzberg restaurant with terrace, serving traditional dishes of the Swabian region (southern Germany).

K8   Fichtestrasse 24   6930101   Daily 6PM–1:30AM   U-Bahn Südstern

GUGELHOF (££)
Popular Prenzlauer Berg restaurant offering Alsatian specialities – try the trout in Riesling. Reservations advised.

L3   Knaackstrasse 37   4429229   Daily 10AM–midnight   U-Bahn Senefelder

HARDTKE (££)

A popular restaurant near the Ku'damm. Standard German cuisine, served in traditional style.

🚹 E7 ✉ Meinekestrasse 27 ☎ 8819827 🕐 Daily 10AM–1AM 🚇 U-Bahn Uhlandstrasse

KAFKA (£)

Meeting-place for well-heeled 20-somethings. Enticing selection of meat and fish dishes includes Argentinian roast beef.

🚹 L7 ✉ Oranienstrasse 204 ☎ 6122429 🕐 Mon–Sun 11AM–1AM. Breakfast 11AM–3PM 🚇 U-Bahn Görlitzer Banhof

LUTTER & WEGNER (£££)

This historic 19th-century restaurant on the Gendarmenmarkt has Austrian cuisine as well as German; also a wine bar.

🚹 J5 ✉ Charlottenstrasse 56 ☎ 20295410 🕐 Daily 11AM–2AM 🚇 U-Bahn Hausvogteiplatz

MARJELLCHEN (££)

Genuine East Prussian cooking at affordable prices. Sorrel soup and Königsberg dumplings are among the specialities.

🚹 C7 ✉ Mommsenstrasse 9 ☎ 8832676 🕐 Daily 5PM–midnight. Closed Sun in summer 🚇 S-Bahn Charlottenburg

OLIVE (£££)

A large, friendly restaurant in Charlottenburg. International dishes as well as German.

🚹 C4 ✉ Tegeler Weg 97 ☎ 3443396 🕐 Daily 11:30AM–1AM 🚇 U-Bahn Mierendorffplatz

RADKE'S GASTHAUS (£££)

Attractive restaurant with old Berlin cooking. Sunday brunch noon to 6PM.

🚹 E7 ✉ Marburger Strasse 16 ☎ 2134652 🕐 Daily 11AM–2AM 🚇 U-Bahn Augsburger Strasse

RESTAURATION 1900 (££)

This classy bistro is a rising star in Prenzlauer Berg's dining scene, so reservations are advised. Food and drink are good, ambience relaxed.

🚹 L3 ✉ Husemannstrasse 1 ☎ 4494052 🕐 Daily 4PM–12:30AM 🚇 U-Bahn Sennefelder Platz

RÜBEZAHL (££)

Homely Berlin cooking served in attractive surroundings with a view of the Müggelsee.

🚹 Off map to southeast ✉ Am Grossen Müggelsee ☎ 658820 🕐 Daily noon–midnight 🚇 S-Bahn Friedrichshagen then tram 60

SPREE-ATHEN (£££)

Cheerful Charlottenburg restaurant that takes a nostalgic look back at the 'good old days' of Wilhelmine Germany.

🚹 D5 ✉ Leibnizstrasse 60 ☎ 3241733 🕐 Mon–Sat 6PM–midnight 🚇 U-Bahn Deutsche Oper

STORCH (££)

A jewel in the crown of Schöneberg restaurants, Storch specialises in Alsatian cuisine. Volker Hauptvogel's virtuoso variations on tarte flambé are a local legend. (No credit cards.)

🚹 F8 ✉ Wartburgstrasse 54 ☎ 7842059 🕐 Daily 6PM–1AM 🚇 U-Bahn Bayerischer Platz

Blockhaus Nikolskoe

This log cabin, situated in secluded woodland, was presented in 1818 by Friedrich Wilhelm III to his daughter and her fiancé, the future Czar Nicholas I of Russia (hence Nikolskoe). A steep climb to the terrace offers breathtaking views across the Havel. The perfectly placed restaurant gets very crowded, so arrive early or book in advance.

INTERNATIONAL RESTAURANTS

Bamberger Reiter

German foodlovers are prepared to travel to visit Franz Raneburger's famous restaurant. Raneburger is Austrian by birth but now regards Berlin as his home. Although he describes his cooking as Austro-Prussian, his culinary creations are by no means confined to the territories of these historic rivals – even the French get a look-in. His goose-liver tarts are an experience not to be missed.

BAMBERGER REITER (£££)

Reservations are essential at this outstanding restaurant (see panel).
✚ E7 ✉ Regensburgerstrasse 7 ☎ 2184282 🕐 Tue–Sat 6PM–1AM 🚇 U-Bahn Spichernstrasse

BORCHARDT (£££)

A smart, 1920s-style restaurant much in favour with fashion-conscious Berliners, who go there for the fine Sunday brunch.
✚ J5 ✉ Französische Strasse 47 ☎ 2293144 🕐 Daily 11:30AM–2AM 🚇 U-Bahn Französische Strasse

CARPE DIEM (££)

A large, boisterous restaurant in a central location. Tables are laid out in the shadows of the S-Bahn arches in summer. (No credit cards.)
✚ D6 ✉ Savigny Passage, Arch 576–7 ☎ 3132728 🕐 Mon–Sat 11AM–1AM 🚇 S-Bahn Savignyplatz

REINHARD'S (££)

This modern, very busy bistro is splendidly located in the sedate rococo Nikolaiviertel, not far from Alexanderplatz.
✚ K5 ✉ Poststrasse 28 ☎ 2425295 🕐 Sun–Thu 9AM–midnight; Fri-Sat 9AM–1AM 🚇 U- or S-Bahn Alexanderplatz

FRENCH

BOVRIL (£££)

Fresh, beautifully presented French-German food in an old bistro setting, popular with businessmen and the literati.
✚ E7 ✉ Ku'damm 184 ☎ 8818461 🕐 Mon–Sat noon–2AM 🚇 U-Bahn Uhlandstrasse

COUR CARRÉE (££)

Travel back in time to *fin-de-siècle* Berlin by eating in this fine restaurant with the bonus of a garden. (No credit cards.)
✚ D6 ✉ Savignyplatz 5 ☎ 3125238 🕐 Daily noon–2AM 🚇 S-Bahn Savignyplatz

FRANZÖSISCHER HOF (£££)

Elegant, with views of the Gendarmenmarkt and Schinkel's magnificent concert hall.
✚ J5 ✉ Jägerstrasse 56 ☎ 2293969 🕐 Daily 11AM–midnight 🚇 U-Bahn Französische Strasse

LE CANARD (£££)

One of the delights of Savignyplatz, Le Canard specialises in authentic southern French cuisine served in a boisterous atmosphere with music.
✚ D7 ✉ Knesebeckstrasse 88 ☎ 3122645 🕐 Mon–Sat 5PM–midnight 🚇 S-Bahn Savignyplatz

PARIS-BAR (££)

A French bistro in the restaurant heartland of Savignyplatz.
✚ D6 ✉ Kantstrasse 152 ☎ 3138052 🕐 Daily noon–1AM 🚇 S-Bahn Savignyplatz

RESTE FIDÈLE (££)

Attractive presentations of French food, with good attentive service.
✚ D6 ✉ Bleibtreustrasse 41 ☎ 8811605 🕐 Sun–Thu 11AM–1AM; Fri, Sat 11AM–2AM 🚇 S-Bahn Savignyplatz

GREEK

ALEXANDER DER GROSSE (££)
Friendly Greek taverna in Kreuzberg. Huge helpings.
➕ N7 ✉ Schlesische Strasse 9 ☎ 6187365
🕐 Daily noon–midnight
🚇 U-Bahn Schlesisches Tor

ITALIAN

BAR CENTRALE (££)
This lively bar-restaurant caters for a stylish business clientele. Good value and attractive presentation (see panel).
➕ H8 ✉ Yorckstrasse 89
☎ 7862989 🕐 Daily 6PM–3AM
🚇 U- or S-Bahn Yorckstrasse

CANDELA (££)
Busy but relaxed Schöneberg restaurant; friendly staff, wholesome Italian cooking. Book at weekends.
➕ F8 ✉ Grunewaldstrasse 81
☎ 7821409 🕐 Daily 5PM–1AM
🚇 U-Bahn Eisenacher Strasse

DON CAMILLO (£££)
The prices reflect the fact that this is one of the most highly regarded Italian restaurants in Berlin. Near Schloss Charlottenburg.
➕ C5 ✉ Schlossstrasse 7
☎ 3223572 🕐 Mon–Sat 6–10:30PM. Closed Sun 🚇 U-Bahn Sophie-Charlotten-Platz

TRATTORIA À MUNTAGNOLA (£££)
The celebrated cook, Mamma Angela, draws from ancient traditional recipes of Muntagnola, in southern Italy.
➕ F7 ✉ Fuggerstrasse 27
☎ 2116642 🕐 Daily noon–midnight 🚇 U-Bahn Nollendorfplatz

TRATTORIA LAPPEGGI (££)
Easy-going Italian restaurant in Prenzlauer Berg. Inventive pasta.
➕ L3 ✉ Kollwitzstrasse 56
☎ 4426347 🕐 Daily noon–midnight 🚇 U-Bahn Senerfelderplatz

MEXICAN

CANTINA MARGARITA (££)
A no-frills Kreuzberg restaurant that's friendly and informal. Thirty types of Margarita cocktail.
➕ L7 ✉ Skalitzer Strasse 73
☎ 6111284 🕐 Daily noon–2AM 🚇 U-Bahn Kottbusser Tor

PORTUGUESE

CARAVELA (£)
Wonderful grilled fish in a southern suburb. Loyal following.
➕ Off map to south
✉ Dickhardtstrasse 27
☎ 8522660 🕐 Daily noon–midnight 🚇 U-Bahn Walther-Schreiber-Platz

LUSIADA (££)
Fish dishes take pride of place in this laid-back Portuguese on Berlin's most famous avenue.
➕ D7 ✉ Ku'damm 132a
☎ 8915869 🕐 Daily 5PM–4AM 🚇 U-Bahn Uhlandstrasse

RUSSIAN

PASTERNAK (££)
Marina Lehmann's delightful restaurant has a literary theme. Reservations advised.
➕ L3 ✉ Knaackstrasse 22–4
☎ 4413399 🕐 Mon–Sat noon–2AM; Sun 10AM–2AM
🚇 U-Bahn Senefelderplatz

Bar Centrale

One of the more enjoyable experiences in Berlin is dining out at the Bar Centrale in Yorckstrasse, a neighbourhood on the fringes of Kreuzberg, favoured by stylish young Berliners. The bar gets crowded so tables spill out on to the pavement and it is easy to see why the place is so popular. The Italian food is beautifully presented, service is courteous, and newspaper vendors drop in with copies of the late evening editions. A grappa rounds off the meal nicely.

ASIAN & VEGETARIAN RESTAURANTS

Maharadscha

Visitors wishing to extend their horizons in an easterly direction might like to try this classical Indian restaurant in the heart of the city. Although the lamb and chicken curries are recommended, aficionados opt for the vegetarian dishes – a great strength of Indian cuisine, deriving from the Hindu outlawing of beef and Muslim proscriptions against pork. Try the *palak panir* (cream cheese with spinach) or the aubergine salad.

CHINESE

HO LIN WAH (£££)
Authentic Chinese dishes served in the opulent but intimate surroundings of a former embassy.
🚇 D7 ✉ Ku'damm 218 ☎ 8823271 🕐 Daily noon–midnight 🚇 U-Bahn Uhlandstrasse

INDIAN

INDIA (££)
Reasonably priced meat and vegetarian dishes.
🚇 J8 ✉ Bergmannstrasse 100 ☎ 6926976 🕐 Daily noon–midnight 🚇 U-Bahn Gneisenaustrasse

MAHARADSCHA (£££)
Vegetarian dishes are the speciality here (see panel).
🚇 F7 ✉ Fuggerstrasse 21 ☎ 2138826 🕐 Daily noon–midnight 🚇 U-Bahn Nollendorfplatz

INDONESIAN

TUK-TUK (££)
Prices have gone up, but the food is still worth it. In Schöneberg.
🚇 G8 ✉ Grossgörschenstrasse 2 ☎ 7811588 🕐 Daily 5:30PM–1AM 🚇 U- or S-Bahn Yorckstrasse

JAPANESE

HAQUIN (£££)
While the setting is nondescript, the Japanese cuisine is second to none.
🚇 F7 ✉ Martin-Luther-Strasse 1 ☎ 2182027 🕐 Fri–Wed 6PM–11:30PM; also weekends and holidays noon–3PM 🚇 U-Bahn Wittenbergplatz

SAPPORO-KAN (£££)
Reserve – these practised purveyors of *sushi* and other Japanese delicacies are popular with Berliners.
🚇 D7 ✉ Schlüterstrasse 52 ☎ 8812973 🕐 Mon–Sat noon–2PM, 6PM–midnight; Sun 6PM–midnight 🚇 S-Bahn Savignyplatz

KOREAN

KWANG JU GRILL (£)
The South Korean chef serves up huge portions of sweet and sour chicken and pork ribs, etc., at very reasonable prices.
🚇 D8 ✉ Emser Strasse 24 ☎ No phone 🕐 Daily noon–midnight; Fri, Sat till 2AM 🚇 U-Bahn Hohenzollernplatz

THAI

FISH AND VEGETABLES (£)
An enterprising Thai fast-food outfit. Try the Viktoriabarsch (perch) in lemon leaves.
🚇 F8 ✉ Goltzstrasse 32 ☎ No phone 🕐 Daily noon–midnight 🚇 U-Bahn Nollendorfplatz

MAO THAI (££)
An intimate cellar restaurant. Try the pineapple and coconut filled with prawns.
🚇 L3 ✉ Wörther Strasse 30 ☎ 4419261 🕐 Daily noon–2:30, 6–11:30 🚇 U-Bahn Senefelderplatz

VEGETARIAN

THÜRNAGEL (££)
A no-frills place serving imaginative vegetarian dishes. (No credit cards.)
🚇 J8 ✉ Gneisenaustrasse 57 ☎ 6914800 🕐 Daily 6–11:30PM 🚇 U-Bahn Gneisenaustrasse

MIDDLE EASTERN, TURKISH & OUT-OF-TOWN RESTAURANTS

MIDDLE EASTERN

BAGDAD (££)
One of Kreuzberg's most popular haunts. The garden is a plus.

✚ N7 ✉ Schlesische Strasse 2 ☎ 6126962 🕔 Daily 4PM–midnight 🚇 U-Bahn Schlesisches Tor

DER ÄGYPTER (££)
One of the few Middle Eastern restaurants in this part of town. Good vegetarian selection.

✚ C6 ✉ Kantstrasse 26 ☎ 3139230 🕔 Daily 5PM–1AM 🚇 U-Bahn Wilmersdorfer Strasse

TURKISH

FOYER (£££)
Classy Anatolian cooking in the centre of town. Try the spicy meatballs with feta cheese filling or aromatic lamb chops.

✚ E6 ✉ Uhlandstrasse 28 ☎ 8814268 🕔 Mon–Sat 5PM–11:30PM 🚇 U-Bahn Uhlandstrasse

ISTANBUL (££)
The food at this well-known establishment is not inexpensive but it *is* guaranteed authentic.

✚ D7 ✉ Knesebeckstrasse 77 ☎ 8832777 🕔 Daily noon–midnight 🚇 S-Bahn Savignyplatz

MERHABA (££)
No frills but this is where the local Turkish community likes to eat.

✚ K8 ✉ Hasenheide 39 ☎ 6921713 🕔 Mon–Sat 4PM–midnight 🚇 U-Bahn Südstern

SONDO (££)
Homely Anatolian cooking in the relaxed surroundings of Prenzlauer Berg. (No credit cards.)

✚ L3 ✉ Husemannstrasse 10 ☎ 4420724 🕔 Daily 5PM–1:30AM 🚇 U-Bahn Eberswalder Strasse

OUT-OF-TOWN

DER KLOSTERKELLER (£££)
A historic restaurant in the centre of town (near the Dutch Quarter) with traditional Prussian food and entertainment.

✚ Off map ✉ Friedrich-Ebert-Strasse 95 ☎ (0331) 291218 🕔 Daily noon–midnight 🚇 S-Bahn Potsdam Stadt

IGEL (££)
A friendly hotel-restaurant with views of the Tegeler See and Havel.

✚ Off map to northwest ✉ Friederikestrasse 33–4 ☎ 4360010 🕔 Daily noon–midnight 🚇 U-Bahn Alt Tegel then bus 222

LORETTA AM WANNSEE (££)
A large garden restaurant, handy for the S-Bahn and next door to the harbour. Grills and fish.

✚ Off map ✉ Kronprinzessinnenweg 260 ☎ 8035156 🕔 Daily 9AM–1AM 🚇 S-Bahn Wannsee

RATSKELLER (££)
Babelsberg's Old Town Hall is the setting for this welcoming cellar restaurant, with traditional German food.

✚ Off map ✉ Karl Liebknecht-Strasse 135 ☎ (0331) 707426 🕔 Daily 11:30AM–midnight 🚇 S-Bahn Bablesberg

Little Istanbul
Kreuzberg boasts the largest Turkish community outside Istanbul. There are dozens of restaurants in the exotic neighbourhoods of Kottbusser Tor and Schlesisches Tor, all offering inexpensive but authentic Anatolian cuisine.

67

CAFÉS

Café Kranzler

The traditional Berlin café is an Austrian import – Johann Georg Kranzler opened his first coffee shop in 1835. Café Kranzler still exists, though it moved west from Unter den Linden to the Ku'damm. Few visitors can resist the intriguing selection of cakes and pastries provocatively displayed in the windows. *Quark-kirschkuchen* (cheesecake with cherries) and *Mokkatorte* (coffeecake) are local favourites. Youngsters tend to go for the multi-flavoured ice-creams.

BARCOMI'S DELI (£)
Friendly courtyard deli with an enticing range of American snacks – everything from bagels to chocolate cake.
+ K4 ✉ Sophienstrasse 21 ☎ 2859836 🕐 Mon–Sat 9AM–10PM; Sun from 10AM 🚇 S-Bahn Hackescher Markt

CAFÉ AEDES (££)
A trendy spot for those who want to see and be seen. There is an art gallery here, too.
+ D6 ✉ Savigny Passage, Arch 599 ☎ 3125504 🕐 Daily 7AM–midnight 🚇 S-Bahn Savignyplatz

CAFÉ BLEIBTREU (£)
Popular with young trendies, this café is convenient for the Savignyplatz nightlife. Appetising buffet breakfast Sat and Sun 9:30AM–3:30PM.
+ D6 ✉ Bleibtreustrasse 45 ☎ 8814756 🕐 Daily 9:30AM–1AM 🚇 S-Bahn Savignyplatz

CAFÉ EINSTEIN (££)
Traditional Viennese-style coffee house trying to re-create a prewar Berlin café atmosphere. There are newspapers and a garden, but prices are steep.
+ F7 ✉ Kurfürstenstrasse 58 ☎ 2615096 🕐 Daily till 2AM 🚇 U-Bahn Kurfurstenstrasse

CAFÉ IM LITERATURHAUS (££)
Relax in the formal, 1890s surroundings of this house. Attractive garden. Some vegetarian dishes.
+ E7 ✉ Fasanenstrasse 23 ☎ 8825414 🕐 Daily 9:30AM–1AM 🚇 U-Bahn Uhlandstrasse

CAFÉ IM MUSEUM DAHLEM (£–££)
A convenient watering hole during, or after, a visit to the Dahlem museums (► 51). Hot meals until 3PM.
+ Off map to south ✉ Lansstrasse 8 ☎ 8314884 🕐 Tue–Fri 9–5; Sat–Sun 10–5 🚇 U-Bahn Dahlem-Dorf

CAFÉ KRANZLER (££)
Still trading successfully on the historic name, though no longer on Unter den Linden. The crowded tables overlook the Ku'damm (see panel).
+ D7 ✉ Ku'damm 18 ☎ 8826911 🕐 Daily 8AM–midnight 🚇 U-Bahn Uhlandstrasse

CAFÉ M (££)
One of Schöneberg's most popular late-night haunts, with nonstop breakfasts. No frills, but plenty of atmosphere.
+ F8 ✉ Goltzstrasse 33 ☎ 2167092 🕐 Daily 9AM–2AM 🚇 U-Bahn Nollendorfplatz

CAFÉ MÖHRING (££)
Quiet and rather formal - perfect for morning coffee. Wide variety of delicious *Torten* and ice-cream.
+ D7 ✉ Ku'damm 213 ☎ 8812075 🕐 Daily 7AM–midnight 🚇 U-Bahn Adenauerplatz

CAFÉ OREN (£)
Light and airy café-restaurant near the Synagogue. An exotic mix of Israeli and Middle Eastern dishes; red wine from the Golan Heights.
+ J4 ✉ Oranienburger Strasse 28 ☎ 2828228 🕐 Daily 10AM–1AM 🚇 S-Bahn Hackescher Markt

CAFÉ ÜBERSEE (£)

Busy through to the early hours, the Übersee is an attractive café in Kreuzberg serving breakfast until 4PM daily.

⊞ L7 ✉ Paul-Lincke-Ufer 44 ☎ 6188765 🕙 Daily 9AM–2AM 🚇 U-Bahn Kottbusser Tor

MARKTHATLLE (£)

This lively café is 'the' meeting place in Kreuzberg. An American breakfast is available all day.

⊞ M7 ✉ Pücklerstrasse 3 ☎ No phone 🕙 Daily 9AM–late 🚇 U-Bahn Gorlitzer Banhof

OPERNPALAIS (£)

Redolent of old Berlin, this palatial café, with an expensive restaurant upstairs, is next to the Staatsoper.

⊞ J5 ✉ Unter den Linden 5 ☎ 2002269 🕙 Daily 11AM–midnight 🚇 U-Bahn Französische Strasse

RESTAURANT EOSANDER (££)

Old sepia photographs line the walls of this turn-of-the-century café just across the road from Schloss Charlottenburg. Children's menu.

⊞ C5 ✉ Spandauer Damm ☎ 3423037 🕙 Daily 8AM–midnight 🚇 U-Bahn Richard-Wagner-Platz

SCHWARZES CAFÉ (££)

Nightclubbers on their way home meet besuited businessmen about to set off for work.

⊞ D6 ✉ Kantstrasse 148 ☎ 3138038 🕙 Daily from 5AM 🚇 S-Bahn Savignyplatz

SOPHIE ECK (££)

Friendly café-restaurant in the shadow of the Sophienkirke. Wide range of reasonably priced German food.

⊞ K4 ✉ Grosse Hamburger Strasse 37 ☎ 2834065 🕙 Daily 10AM–1AM 🚇 S-Bahn Hackescher Markt

TADSCHIKISCHE TEESTUBE (£)

A strictly no-smoking tea house where footsore visitors to the Mitte can kick off their shoes and loll on traditional Tadzhik divans.

⊞ J5 ✉ Unter den Linden (behind the Neue Wache) ☎ No phone 🕙 Mon–Fri 5PM–midnight; Sat–Sun 3PM–midnight 🚌 Bus 100

TIM'S CANADIAN DELI (£)

Busy café convenient to the weekend market on Winterfeldplatz. Brownies and muffins.

⊞ F7 ✉ Maassenstrasse 14 ☎ 21756960 🕙 Mon–Sat 8AM–midnight; Sun from 9AM 🚇 U-Bahn Nollendorfplatz

YORCKSCHLÖSSCHEN (£)

A busy locals' café with an extensive breakfast menu.

⊞ J8 ✉ Yorckstrasse 15 ☎ 2158070 🕙 Daily 9AM–late 🚇 U-Bahn Mehringdamm

ZUM NUSSBAUM (£)

'The Nut Tree' is a traditional Berlin Gasthaus situated near Fischerinsel in the prettily renovated Nikolaiviertel.

⊞ K5 ✉ Probstrasse ☎ 2423095 🕙 Daily noon–2AM 🚇 U- or S-Bahn Alexanderplatz

Breakfast in Berlin

For Berliners, breakfast almost amounts to a way of life. You can, it seems, take the meal at any time of the day, and you can spend as long over it as you like. Ham and eggs, sausage, cheese, muesli, pumpernickel and even cakes may be on the agenda for the calorie-challenged Berliner. On the basis of 'if you can't beat them, join them,' why not pop in to one of the many establishments specialising in this heartwarming repast?

DEPARTMENT STORES & SOUVENIRS

Museum mementoes

Like it or not, the vexing question of what to take home for absent friends and relatives cannot be put off for ever. One suggestion for harassed last-minute present buyers is the Gipsformerei, the museum shop at Schloss Charlottenburg, which that specialises in plaster casts of famous museum exhibits. That bust of Queen Nefertiti would add a touch of class to the cabinet back home – why not treat yourself?

Shopping hours

Most shops open between 9 and 10 and close at 6 or 6:30. Many are closed on Saturday afternoon. Unusual hours are indicated in individual entries.

GALERIES LAFAYETTE
Branch of the Parisian shopping mecca – an architectural treat too.
➕ J5 ✉ Französischestrasse 23 ☎ 209480 ⏰ Mon–Fri 9:30AM–8PM; Sat 9AM–4PM 🚇 U-Bahn Französische Strasse

GIPSFORMEREI
This unusual workshop sells plaster models of Nefertiti, Tutankhamun and other stars of the state museums (see panel).
➕ B5 ✉ Sophie-Charlotten-Strasse 17–18 ☎ 3217011 ⏰ Closed Sat 🚇 U-Bahn Sophie-Charlotten-Platz

HERTIE
This branch of the Hertie chain is a reliable source of everyday household items at reasonable prices.
➕ D7 ✉ Kurfürstendamm 231 ☎ 880030 🚇 U-Bahn Uhlandstrasse

INFO-BOX
A full selection of souvenirs, books, etc., on the theme of Berlin, its history and architecture.
➕ H6 ✉ Stresemann Strasse/Potsdamer Platz ☎ 2266240 ⏰ Daily 9AM–7PM 🚇 S- or U-Bahn Potsdamer Platz

INFORMATION OFFICE, BERLIN TOURISMUS MARKETING
Excellent selection of typical Berlin souvenirs
➕ E6 ✉ Budapester Strasse 45 ☎ 250025 ⏰ Mon–Sat 8AM–10PM; Sun 9AM–9PM 🚇 U- or S-Bahn Zoologischer Garden

KADEWE (KAUFHAUS DES WESTENS)
The second largest department store in the world (after Harrods of London), KaDeWe claims to stock more than 250,000 items. The Food Hall is a must (► 75).
➕ F7 ✉ Tauentzienstrasse 27 ☎ 21210 ⏰ Late opening Thu to 8:30 🚇 U-Bahn Wittenbergplatz

KARSTADT
One of several Karstadt department stores in Berlin, this branch is in the fashionable Charlottenburg district.
➕ C6 ✉ Wilmersdorfer Strasse 109 ☎ 31891 🚇 U-Bahn Wilmersdorfer Strasse

KAUFHOF
This western department store occupies the premises of an outmoded East German predecessor.
➕ L4 ✉ Alexanderplatz ☎ 24640 🚇 U- or S-Bahn Alexanderplatz

QUELLE
A department store in Wedding that stocks the usual household items.
➕ G2 ✉ Müller Strasse 153 ☎ 4650980 🚇 U- Bahn Leopoldplatz

SCENARIO
A quirky shop selling wacky gifts and souvenirs, leatherware, stationery, cards and fun jewellery.
➕ D6 ✉ Savigny Passage, Arch 602 ☎ 3129199 🚇 S-Bahn Savignyplatz

WERTHEIM
Traditional department store with a wide range of gifts bearing the Berlin logo – T-shirts, mugs, etc. Near the Kaiser-Wilhelm-Gedächtniskirche.
➕ E7 ✉ Ku'damm 231 ☎ 880030 🚇 U-Bahn Kurfürstendamm

BOUTIQUES & DESIGNER CLOTHES

BLEIBGRÜN
Purveyors of designer shoes and bags with much-sought-after labels.
✚ D7 ✉ Bleibtreustrasse 27 ☎ 8850080 Ⓜ U-Bahn Uhlandstrasse

EISDIELER
This shop is a showcase for young Berlin designers.
✚ J4 ✉ Auguststrasse 74 Ⓜ U-Bahn Oranienburger Tor

GIANNI VERSACE
Berlins's outlet for the latest fashions from the house of the famous Italian designer.
✚ D7 ✉ Kurfürstendamm 185 ☎ 885740 Ⓜ U-Bahn Uhlandstrasse

HELLMANN POUR ELLE
One of a chain of five shops owned by Patrick Hellmann with fashion items aimed at the sophisticated and well-heeled shopper. Gaultier and Calvin Klein are represented. Expect to spend accordingly.
✚ E7 ✉ Fasanenstrasse 26 ☎ 8824201 Ⓜ U- Bahn Uhlandstrasse

JIL SANDER
Understated but eye-catching fashions from this celebrity German designer.
✚ D7 ✉ Kurfürstendamm 185 ☎ 8867020 Ⓜ U-Bahn Uhlandstrasse

KOSTÜMHAUS
The sound of sewing machines rattling away in the background is acoustic proof that the ladieswear is tailored on the premises.
✚ K4 ✉ Rosenthaler Strasse 40–1 ☎ 2827018 Ⓜ S-Bahn Hackescher Markt

KRAMBERG
All the top designer names are represented in this shop, which appeals to fashion sophisticates of both sexes.
✚ D7 ✉ Ku'damm 56–7 ☎ 3279010 Ⓜ U-Bahn Adenauerplatz

LISA D
Popular boutique in the renovated Hackesche Höfe.
✚ K4 ✉ Rosenthaler Strasse 40–1 ☎ 2829061 Ⓜ S-Bahn Hackescher Markt

MIKES LADEN
This shop sells international fashions for both men and women.
✚ E7 ✉ Nürnberger Strasse 50–6 ☎ 2182020 Ⓜ U-Bahn Augsburger Strasse

NIX
Chic fashions for men and women. The shop is located in Mitte.
✚ J4 ✉ Auguststrasse 86 ☎ 2818044 Ⓜ U-Bahn Oranienburger Tor

OFFERMANN
This emporium sells leatherware and accessories. On the Ku'damm.
✚ D7 ✉ Kurfürstendamm 201 ☎ 8852732 Ⓜ U-Bahn Uhlandstrasse

City originals
Where fashion is concerned, Berlin is not a city you would mention in the same breath as London, Milan or Paris but Berliners are as style-conscious as the inhabitants of any cosmopolitan city. The boutiques off the Ku'damm, for example in Knesebeckstrasse, Uhlandstrasse or Pariserstrasse, include some of the city's home fashion houses, promoting the creations of Patrick Hellmann, Jutta Meierling and others.

SECOND-HAND & OFF-BEAT

The alternative scene

Berlin's chic cosmopolitan image is constantly being undermined by a brazenly nonconformist alternative with roots in the 1960s. There is plenty of evidence of the latter in the remarkable variety of stores specialising in second-hand and off-beat clothing and jewellery. You can have great fun inspecting the wares. A good starting point is the Garage, which sells used clothes by the kilo. The more discerning should sample Kaufhaus Schrill.

AVE MARIA
Devotional statues and Kitsch items compete here with clothing for men, women and children.
✚ G7 ✉ Potsdamer Strasse 75 ☎ No phone 🚇 U-Bahn Kurfürstenstrasse

GARAGE
A large warehouse by Nollendorfplatz U-Bahn station, claiming to be Europe's biggest second-hand store. Clothes are sold by weight.
✚ F7 ✉ Ahornstrasse 2 ☎ 2112760 🚇 U-Bahn Nollendorfplatz

KANT STORE
For shoppers with an unconventional taste. Cowboy boots and leather leggings are among the items on sale.
✚ D6 ✉ Kantstrasse 33 ☎ 3135640 🚇 S-Bahn Savignyplatz

KAUFHAUS SCHRILL
Showy fashion accessories – everything from hats and gloves to ties and jewellery. The roll call of former patrons is said to include Sylvester Stallone.
✚ D6 ✉ Bleibtreustrasse 46 ☎ 8824048 🚇 S-Bahn Savignyplatz

KNOPF-PAUL
The ingenious owner of this Kreuzberg shop can make buttons out of everything – even plum stones and typewriter keys.
✚ J8 ✉ Zossener Strasse 10 ☎ 6921212 🚇 U-Bahn Gneisenaustrasse

MADE IN BERLIN
This unusual shop sells second-hand clothes of quality, including 1920s cocktail dresses and tuxedos from the 1950s.
✚ G8 ✉ Potsdamer Strasse 106 ☎ 2622431 🚇 U-Bahn Kurfürstenstrasse

RIO
This exclusive store near Savignyplatz specialises in sophisticated costume jewellery by Lagerfeld and Montana.
✚ D6 ✉ Bleibtreustrasse 52 ☎ 3133152 🚇 S-Bahn Savignyplatz

SCHWARZE MODE
'Black Fashion' appeals to shoppers with a taste for latex and leather.
✚ F8 ✉ Grunewaldstrasse 91 ☎ 7845922 🚇 U-Bahn Eisenacher Strasse

SPITZE
Glamorous clothes, accessories and handicrafts spanning the period 1860–1960.
✚ D6 ✉ Weimarer Strasse 19 ☎ 316068 🚇 U-Bahn Deutsche Oper

WAAHNSINN BERLIN
Fashion and oddities from the 1920s to the 1970s including handspun tops from Bali.
✚ K5 ✉ Neue Promenade 3 ☎ 2820029 🚇 S-Bahn Hackescher Markt

WARNER BROS. STUDIO STORE
On sale here are ties, cufflinks, etc., with Bugs Bunny, Tweety, Road Runner motifs.
✚ E7 ✉ Tauentzienstrasse 9 ☎ 25454401 🚇 U-Bahn Kurfürstendamm

GALLERIES

DAAD
Avant-garde and modern art.
✚ F5 ✉ Kurfürstenstrasse 58
☎ 2613640 🚌 Bus 100

GALERIE BREMER
A long-established gallery that exhibits the work of contemporary German artists, including relative newcomers. A bar opens in the evenings.
✚ E7 ✉ Fasanenstrasse 37
☎ 8814908 🕐 Tue–Fri noon–6; Sat 11–1 🚇 U-Bahn Uhlandstrasse

GALERIE BRUSBERG
If you are into Dada and surrealist art, then this is the place to come. You might even be lucky enough to spot the occasional Picasso or Miró.
✚ E7 ✉ Ku'damm 213
☎ 8827682 🕐 Tue–Fri 10–6:30; Sat 10–2 🚇 U-Bahn Uhlandstrasse

GALERIA GROTH
Among the pieces exhibited here are reproductions of pre-Columbian objects from Bogotá.
✚ E7 ✉ Uhlandstrasse 170 (passage) ☎ 8818161
🚇 U-Bahn Uhlandstrasse

GALERIE PELS-LEUSDEN
Located in the beautiful former home of turn-of-the-century architect Hans Grisebach, and devoted mainly to international art of the 19th and 20th centuries.
✚ E7 ✉ Fasanenstrasse 25
☎ 8859150 🕐 Mon–Fri 10–6:30, Sat 10–2 🚇 U-Bahn Uhlandstrasse

GALERIE SPRINGER
Right up to date with trends in modern German art, both painting and photography.
✚ E6 ✉ Fasanenstrasse 13
☎ 3127063 🕐 Mon–Fri 10–7; Sat 11–2 🚇 U-Bahn Uhlandstrasse

GALERIE WOHNMASCHINE
Promotes the work of up-and-coming but impoverished artists.
✚ J4 ✉ Tucholskystrasse 34
☎ 2815812 🕐 Tue, Wed, Fri, Sat 2–7; Thu 5–9 🚇 S-Bahn Oranienburger Strasse

HACKESCHE HÖFE
Now smartened up, these historic courtyards remain at the heart of Berlin's contemporary art scene.
✚ K4 ✉ Rosenthaler Strasse
☎ No phone 🚇 S-Bahn Hackescher Markt

KUNST-WERKE BERLIN
Experimental and avant-garde art in one of August-strasse's new galleries.
✚ J4 ✉ Augustrasse 69
☎ 2817325 🚇 S-Bahn Oranienburger Strasse

LINDEN TUNNEL
Weird and wonderful open-air exhibition at the entrance to a former tram tunnel.
✚ J5 ✉ Next to Maxim-Gorki Theatre ☎ No phone
🚌 Bus 100

TACHELES
Splendidly dilapidated Tacheles remain a centre for off-beat and experimental art.
✚ J4 ✉ Oranienburger Strasse 54–6 ☎ 2826185
🚇 S-Bahn Oranienburger Strasse

Art of all kinds

Artists generally divide into the up-and-coming and those who have already made it. The exclusive private galleries around Fasanenstrasse promote the work of established German artists while also exhibiting some of the best in international modern art. The other side of the coin is the crumbling ateliers and studios of Kreuzberg and the Scheunenviertel where the undiscovered, neglected and uncompromising show off their work.

ANTIQUES, GLASS & PORCELAIN

Royal porcelain

Berlin's historic association with porcelain dates from 1763 when Frederick the Great founded the Königliche Porzellan Manufaktor (Royal Porcelain Factory or KPM). It is still going strong today. The firm's principal outlet (with showroom) is on the Ku'damm but the famous KPM hallmark crops up all over the city. The best place to see the historic pieces is the Belvedere at Schloss Charlottenburg (➤ 32).

ANTIQUE LAMPEN
The name of this Charlottenburg emporium says it all. Old lamps, including genuine art-deco and Victorian models, restored to pristine condition, are available – at a price.
✚ C7 ✉ Gervinusstrasse 15
☎ 2233427 🚇 S-Bahn Charlottenburg

ART 1900
Specialist dealers in Jugendstil and Art Deco – pictures, porcelain, lamps, furniture and jewellery.
✚ E7 ✉ Kurfürstendamm 53
☎ 8815627 🚇 U-Bahn Kurfürstendamm

ART & INDUSTRY
Furniture, lamps and accessories in Bauhaus and other functionalist styles. Also watches.
✚ D7 ✉ Bleibtreustrasse 40
☎ 8834946 🚇 S-Bahn Savignyplatz

GLÄSER JAN HINRICHS
A must if you are looking for glassware and don't want to pay through the nose. Prices are more affordable than most and the selection is good.
✚ D7 ✉ Knesebeckstrasse 13–14 ☎ 3131037
🚇 S-Bahn Savignyplatz

KPM
Quality porcelain bearing the renowned KPM hallmark (see panel).
✚ C7 ✉ Ku'damm 26a
☎ 8811802 🚇 U-Bahn Adenauerplatz

MEISSENER PORZELLAN
Porcelain figurines and other decorative items made of the Meissen Porcelain.
✚ D7 ✉ Kurfürstendamm 24
☎ 8819158 🚇 U-Bahn Uhlandstrasse
Also at:
✚ J5 ✉ Unter den Linden 39B
☎ 8819158 🚌 Bus 100

ROSENTHAL STUDIO
An outlet for porcelain and glassware produced by some of the world's most creative designers, including Rosenthal.
✚ E7 ✉ Ku'damm 226
☎ 856340 🚇 U-Bahn Kurfürstendamm

RUSSISCHE SAMOWARE
Beautiful antique Russian Samovars dating back to before the Revolution.
✚ E7 ✉ Marburger Strasse 6
☎ 2113666 🚇 U-Bahn Augsburger Strasse

SEIDEL UND SOHN
Antiques shop specialising in Biedermeier furniture and household items.
✚ F8 ✉ Eisenacher Strasse 13 ☎ 2161850 🚇 U-Bahn Eisenacher Strasse

WILHELM WEIK
Furniture, paintings, and porcelain of the 18th–19th centuries. In the centre of Berlin's antique district.
✚ F7 ✉ Eisenacher Strasse 10
☎ 6061837 🚇 U-Bahn Viktoria-Luise-Platz

YOKOHAMA HAUS
The Meissen porcelain on sale here is a long-established rival of the famous KPM of Berlin.
✚ E7 ✉ Keithstrasse 10
☎ 2183135 🚇 U-Bahn Wittenbergplatz

MARKETS & FOODSHOPS

ANTIK UND FLOHMARKT

Affordable antiques and bric-à-brac under the railway arches of Friedrichstrasse station.

➕ J5   ✉ Friedrichstrasse Bahnhof   ☎ 21502129
🕐 Wed–Mon 11–6
🚇 U- or S-Bahn Friedrichstrasse

BERLINER KUNST-UND-NOSTALGIE-MARKT

Art and nostalgia – for the most part paintings, drawings and antiques.

➕ J5   ✉ Am Zeughaus/Unter den Linden   🕐 Sat–Sun 11–5
🚇 U- or S-Bahn Friedrichstrasse

ENOTECA WEINE

Proprietor Werner Blanck is a great connoisseur of Italian wines.

➕ D8   ✉ Holsteinische Strasse 22   ☎ 8736061
🚇 U-Bahn Hohenzollernplatz

FLOHMARKT

Genuine bargains at knockdown prices in the Tacheles building.

➕ J4   ✉ Oranienburger Strasse   🕐 Sat–Sun 8AM–3PM
🚇 S-Bahn Oranienburger Strasse

KADEWE FOOD HALL

Europe's largest delicatessen. Food and drink from around the world: lobster and caviar, exotic vegetables and spices – and over 1,000 varieties of German sausage.

✉ Sixth floor, KaDeWe (➤ 70)

KING'S TEAGARTEN

More than 200 varieties of tea from all over the world, and classical music to enjoy as well.

➕ D7   ✉ Ku'damm 217
☎ 8837059   🕐 Daily 9–7

🚇 U-Bahn Uhlandstrasse

LA FROMAGERIE

The French proprietor of this tiny Kreuzberg shop tempts customers with more than 40 different unpasteurised cheeses, matured with the help of brine and even beer.

➕ J8   ✉ Gneisenaustrasse 24
☎ 6922579   🚇 U-Bahn Gneisenaustrasse

SIKASSO MARKT

Every conceivable ingredient used in African cooking – palm oil, yams, millet, dried fish, Berber spices and Masai tea.

➕ L6   ✉ Dresdener Strasse 124   ☎ 6148729   🚇 U-Bahn Moritzplatz

STRASSE DES 17 JUNI

A market in the Tiergarten popular with antiques dealers and tourists.

➕ E5   ☎ 3228199
🕐 Weekends   🚇 S-Bahn Tiergarten

TURKISH MARKET

An intriguing market offering choice ethnic food, including olives, cheeses and spiced chicken, in the heart of the Turkish community.

➕ L8   ✉ Maybachufer
☎ 68092926   🕐 Tue–Fri noon–6:30   🚇 U-Bahn Schönleinstrasse

WINTERFELDTMARKT

A favourite with Berliners, this Schöneberg market is one of the city's liveliest. Take brunch in one of the many local cafés (see panel).

➕ F7   ✉ Winterfeldtplatz
🕐 Wed and Sat 8–1
🚇 U-Bahn Nollendorfplatz

Winterfeldtplatz

One pleasant way to while away a Saturday morning is to explore the antiques shops around Motzstrasse, before homing in on one of Berlin's most colourful and entertaining street markets, in Winterfeldtplatz. You never know quite what you will find here, which is the main attraction – everything from hand-me-down jewellery to books with faded covers, and from flowers to children's clothes. Having worked up an appetite, visit one of the numerous cafés serving breakfast in the vicinity – try Tim's Canadian Deli (➤ 69).

THE BEST OF THE REST

Friedrichstrasse

Rebuilt almost from scratch during the last decade, Friedrichstrasse is rapidly becoming a magnet for discerning shoppers, especially aficionados of the latest designer fashions. Galeries Layfayette, also here, is the first branch of the famous department store outside France. Apart from Jean Nouvel's highly innovative open-plan design, the main talking point is the mouth-watering Food Hall, selling everything from pâtés to oysters.

ARARAT

If you want a postcard to send home, look no further. Ararat's selection is vast. The historical views are especially good.
🕂 D6 ✉ Kantstrasse 135 ☎ 3124445 🚇 S-Bahn Savignyplatz

BERLINER ZINNFIGUREN

A magical collection of handmade tin soldiers; also dancing couples, circus animals and other delightful figurines. Justly famous.
🕂 D7 ☎ 3130802 ✉ Knesebeckstrasse 88 🚇 S-Bahn Savignyplatz

CONDOMI

Berliners have never been shy about sex…
🕂 D6 ✉ Kantstrasse 131 ☎ 3135051 🚇 S-Bahn Savignyplatz

DER RIOJA WEINSPEZIALIST

The 'Rioja Specialist' stocks all varieties of wines originating in the Iberian Peninsula.
🕂 G8 ✉ Akazienstrasse 13 ☎ 7822578 🚇 U-Bahn Kleistpark

DER TEELADEN

Berlin's largest tea emporium.
🕂 D7 ✉ Kurfürstendamm 209 ☎ 4423974 🚇 U-Bahn Uhlandstrasse

EUROPA-CENTER

Not only an entertainments complex, the Europa-Center is also Berlin's largest and best-known indoor shopping centre. There are more than 100 outlets in all, on three floors, and there are bars and coffee shops to relax in when the shopping is done.
🕂 E6 ✉ Tauentzienstrasse 🚇 U-Bahn Kurfürstendamm

J UND M FÄSSLER

Stocks a wide selection of toys, souvenirs and curiosities.
🕂 E6 ✉ Europa-Center, Tauentzienstrasse ☎ 2614807 🚇 U-Bahn Kurfürstendamm

KIEPERT

The city's largest collection of books about Berlin.
🕂 E6 ✉ Hardenbergstrasse 4–5 ☎ 3110090 🚇 U-Bahn Zoologischer Garten
Also at:
🕂 J5 ✉ Friedrichstrasse 63 🚇 U- or S-Bahn Friedrichstrasse

KULTURKAUFHAUS

This enormous bookstore in the heart of the Mitte also has huge stocks of videos, CDs and computer software. There is also a 'cookie café'.
🕂 J5 ✉ Friedrichstrasse 90 ☎ 20251111 🚇 U- or S-Bahn Friedrichstrasse

KUNSTBUCHHAND-LUNG GALERIE 2000

Art books from all over the world.
🕂 D5 ✉ Knesebeckstrasse 56–8 ☎ 8838467 🚇 U–Bahn Uhlandstrasse

MAISON DE LA DANSE

Purveyors of all kinds of dancewear, from tutus to tango dresses.
🕂 D6 ✉ Pestalozzistrasse 60 ☎ 3232043 🚇 S-Bahn Savignyplatz

MARGA SCHOELLER

The best selection of fiction and nonfiction books in English in Berlin.
✚ D7 ✉ Knesebeckstrasse 33–4 ☎ 8811112 🔘 S-Bahn Savignyplatz

MAUERSPECHT'S STAATSAUFLÖSUNG

The only place in Berlin where you can still find an authentic piece of the Wall; also GDR and Soviet Union medals, military insignia, etc.
✚ J6 ✉ Friedrichstrasse 44 ☎ 2537250 🔘 U-Bahn Kochstrasse

MUSIKANTIQUARIAT ROBERT HARTWIG

Musical, theatrical and film ephemera.
✚ D6 ✉ Pestalozzistrasse 23 ☎ 3129124 🔘 S-Bahn Savignyplatz

MUSIKHAUS RIEDL

Classical music (CDs, tapes and cheap music).
✚ J5 ✉ Koncerthaus am Gendarmenmarkt ☎ 8827395 🔘 U-Bahn Stadtmitte

MUSIKMARKT SCHALLPLATTEN

Rare vinyl, including hits from the DDR era.
✚ J5 ✉ Friedrichstrasse 165 ☎ 2291475 🔘 U-Bahn Französische Strasse

PARFUM NACH GEWICHT 'PERFUME BY WEIGHT'

A perfumery with a difference: all the scents are homemade. The staff will fill a bottle with the fragrance of your choice – or you can mix your own.
✚ D6 ✉ Kantstrasse 106 ☎ 3243582 🔘 U-Bahn Wilmersdorfer Strasse

POSTERGALERIE 200

The emphasis here is on the quirky and offbeat.
✚ E7 ✉ Ku'damm 195 ☎ 8821959 🔘 U-Bahn Kurfürstendamm

SKI HÜTTE

If you have the sudden urge to play tennis or to go sailing on the Havel, you can be fitted out here. Every type of sports equipment.
✚ E6 ✉ Joachimstalerstrasse 42 ☎ 8811480 🔘 U- or S-Bahn Zoologischer Garten

STROH-KUNSTHANDWERK

Handmade toys and traditional crafts near the Hackescher Höfe.
✚ K4 ✉ Sophienstrasse 9 ☎ 2826754 🔘 S-Bahn Hackescher Markt

TATORT: BUCHHANDLUNG

The 'Scene of the Crime' Bookstore has a large selection of crime novels in various languages.
✚ F7 ✉ Motzstrasse 65 ☎ 2115599 🔘 U-Bahn Nollendorfplatz

THE BRITISH BOOKSHOP

Wide selection of English-language books.
✚ J5 ✉ Mauerstrasse 83–4 ☎ 2384680 🔘 U-Bahn Mohrenstrasse

WIEDENHOFF

Browse among the Solingen cutlery, replica swords, helmets, armour and decorative weapons.
✚ E6 ✉ Europa-Center, Tauentzienstrasse ☎ 2612730 🔘 U-Bahn Kufürstendamm

Europa-Center

There are more than 100 shops in the high-rise shopping mall known as the Europa-Center. The Mercedes star on the roof is something of a landmark and when you have finished your shopping you can take the lift to the viewing platform on the 22nd floor for unbeatable views of Berlin. There is a tourist information office here, too, and you may find yourself returning in the evening to the disco, cinema or cabaret theatre.

THEATRES & CONCERTS

Deutsche Staatsoper

The handsome neo-classical building dominating Bebelplatz is Berlin's oldest opera house, the Deutsche Staatsoper, built in the reign of Frederick the Great. It is currently engaged in a life-and-death struggle with its chief rival, the Deutsche Oper, for fast-disappearing subsidies. The roll-call of musicians who have directed here in the past is amazing — it includes the composers Mendelssohn, Meyerbeer, Liszt and Richard Strauss, the legendary conductor Wilhelm Furtwängler and, more recently, the pianist Daniel Barenboim.

BERLINER ENSEMBLE

Playwright Bertolt Brecht founded this famous theatre company in 1948. Brecht's plays are still in the repertoire, and the theatre recently celebrated his centenary.

J4 Bertolt-Brecht-Platz
2823160 U- or S-Bahn Friedrichstrasse

DEUTSCHE OPER BERLIN

Opera and modern ballet in an uninspired postwar concert hall.

C6 Bismarckstrasse 35
3410249 U-Bahn Deutsche Oper

DEUTSCHE STAATSOPER

Opera and ballet in a beautiful baroque concert hall now restored after extensive wartime bomb damage (see panel).

J5 Unter den Linden 7
2004762 U-Bahn Französische Strasse

DEUTSCHES THEATER

The name of theatre director Max Reinhardt was virtually synonymous with the life of this theatre from the turn of the century until the Nazis came to power. Film stars Pola Negri and Marlene Dietrich performed here.

H4 Schumannstrasse 13
28441225 U-Bahn Oranienburger Tor

KOMISCHE OPER

Operettas and ballet performed in a modern theatre in the Mitte district.

J5 Behrenstrasse 55–7
2292555 U- or S-Bahn Friedrichstrasse

METROPOL-THEATER

Musicals, shows and operettas strong in the heart of the Mitte.

J5 Friedrichstrasse 101
20364117 U- or S-Bahn Friedrichstrasse

PHILHARMONIE

One of the world's most famous orchestras, the Berlin Philharmonic, performs in Hans Scharoun's 1960s architectural masterpiece in the Kulturforum. The acoustics are impeccable, but tickets are as rare as gold dust.

G6 Matthäikirchstrasse 1 254880 U- or S-Bahn Potsdamer Platz

SCHAUSPIELHAUS BERLIN

The magnificent concert hall of the Berlin Symphony Orchestra was designed by architect Karl Friedrich Schinkel in 1818.

J5 Gendarmenmarkt 2
203092102 U-Bahn Französische Strasse

THEATER DES WESTENS

Broadway shows and musicals.

E6 Kantstrasse 12
8822888 U- or S-Bahn Zoologischer Garten

UFA-FABRIK

A well-known spot for alternative music, dance, film and theatre in Kreuzberg. Popular with young Berliners.

Off map to south
Viktoriastrasse 13
755030 U-Bahn Ullsteinstrasse

CABARET

BAR JEDER VERNUNFT

Eat, drink and enjoy the show – there's also a piano bar.

✚ E7 ✉ Schaperstrasse 24
☎ 8831582 🚇 U-Bahn Augsburger Strasse

CHAMÄLEON VARIETÉ

Variety at its most expansive in an art-deco setting. Clowns, acrobats, magicians, etc.; much loved by Berliners.

✚ K4 ✉ Rosenthaler Strasse 40–1 ☎ 2827118
🚇 S-Bahn Hackescher Markt

CHEZ NOUS

Famous for its transvestite shows, and going strong for more than 30 years. Reservations strongly advised.

✚ E7 ✉ Marburger Strasse 14 ☎ 2131810 🚇 U-Bahn Kurfürstendamm

DISTEL

'The Thistle' club is known for its acerbic political satire.

✚ J5 ✉ Friedrichstrasse 101
☎ 2004704 🚇 U- or S-Bahn Friedrichstrasse

FRIEDRICHSTADT-PALAST

The most famous nightspot in eastern Berlin, with a long tradition. The entertainment in the main revue includes variety acts, a floor show and loud music; the small revue is more intimate.

✚ J5 ✉ Friedrichstrasse 107
☎ 28466207 🚇 U- or S-Bahn Friedrichstrasse

LA VIE EN ROSE

Glamorous showgirls in feathers and pearls sing their hearts out.

✚ E6 ✉ Europa-Center
☎ 3236006 🚇 U-Bahn Kurfürstendamm

KABARETT DIE STACHELSCHWEINE

The political satire here is tame and barely merits the prickly associations in the name (*Stachelschwein* means porcupine).

✚ E6 ✉ Europa-Center
☎ 2614795 🚇 U-Bahn Kurfürstendamm

KABARETT DIE WÜHLMÄUSE

'The Voles' offers some of the best and sharpest political satire in Berlin.

✚ E7 ✉ Nürnburger Strasse 33 ☎ 2137047
🚇 U-Bahn Augsburger Strasse

MEHRINGHOF THEATER

A Kreuzberg theatre specialising in radical or 'alternative' cabaret.

✚ J8 ✉ Gneisenaustrasse 2a
☎ 6915099 🚇 U-Bahn Gneisenaustrasse

WINTERGARTEN VARIETE

Long synonymous with late-night entertainment, the Wintergarten guarantees a fun-packed evening starring international enter-tainers from the variety world.

✚ G7
✉ Potsdamerstrasse 96
☎ 2500880 🚇 U-Bahn Kurfürstenstrasse

Goodbye to cabaret?

The 1920s was the undisputed golden age of cabaret, a fact seized upon by Bob Fosse in his 1972 film musical *Cabaret*, based on Christopher Isherwood's novel *Goodbye to Berlin*. The main characteristics of the art form – biting political satire and unabashed sexual licence – aroused the wrath of the Nazi ideologues, who closed down the theatres and arrested many of the performers. Since the war, Berliners have done their best to revive the tradition but the modern clubs are often more akin to variety shows – the bite is missing.

79

PUBS, BARS & CLUBS

Local Tipples

A favourite local drink is Berliner Weisse, beer with a dash of raspberry or woodruff syrup (*mit grün*) – addictive if you have a sweet tooth. This is a traditional beverage; more trendy is *herva mit Mosel*, a peculiar blend of white wine with maté tea that Berliners consume at least half a million times annually, according to recent accounts. Hardened drinkers prefer *Korn* (frothy beer with a schnapps chaser).

BIG EDEN

Once famous for the international celebrities who used to drop in, Big Eden is now a conventional dance club attracting mainly local teenagers and equally youthful visitors.

✚ D7 ✉ Ku'damm 202 ☎ 8826120 🕐 Nightly from 7 Ⓤ U-Bahn Kurfürstendamm

BONNIE AND CLYDE

Prenzlauer Berg bar with old Harley-Davidson cylinders as beer pumps and wide armchairs removed from a tour bus.

✚ L3 ✉ Danziger Strasse 36 ☎ 4409767 🕐 Daily 6PM–late Ⓤ U-Bahn Eberswalder Strasse

COCKTAILBAR X

Increasingly popular east end venue for young trendsetters.

✚ L2 ✉ Raumerstrasse 17 ☎ 4434904 🕐 Daily 6PM–late Ⓤ U-Bahn Eberswalder Strasse

DOLMEN

Lively nightspot featuring DJs and live bands.

✚ K4 ✉ Shönhauser Allee 6–7 ☎ 4406030 🕐 Thu–Sat 11PM–5AM Ⓤ U-Bahn Rosa Luxemburg Platz

FAR OUT

A conventional nightclub in Berlin's west end. The music tends to be mainstream rock and pop.

✚ D7 ✉ Ku'damm 156 ☎ 32000723 🕐 Tue–Sun 10PM–late Ⓤ U-Bahn Adenauerplatz

FOGO

A Kreuzberg establishment that draws an interesting, mainly young crowd.

✚ J8 ✉ Arndstrasse 29 ☎ 6921465 🕐 Daily 8:30PM–6AM Ⓤ U-Bahn Gneisenaustrasse

GAINSBOURG

Named after the famous 1960s French singer, this nightclub plays a raunchy selection of French music.

✚ D6 ✉ Savignyplatz 5 ☎ 3137464 🕐 Daily 5PM–3AM Ⓢ S-Bahn Savignyplatz

HARRY'S NEW YORK BAR

This piano bar in the Hotel Esplanade attracts a mainly business clientele and is suitably restrained.

✚ G6 ✉ Lützowufer 15 ☎ 254780/261011 🕐 Daily noon–3AM Ⓤ U-Bahn Kurfürstenstrasse

JAMES-JOYCE-TAVERN

Guinness and Irish whiskey in a folksy atmosphere.

✚ C7 ✉ Joachim-Friedrich-Strasse 30 ☎ 8917906 🕐 Daily 5PM–2AM Ⓢ S-Bahn Charlottenburg

LEYDICKE

One of the oldest pubs in Berlin, dating from 1877, and among the most atmospheric. The liqueurs and unusually flavoured wines (cherry, gooseberry, etc.) are justly celebrated.

✚ G8 ✉ Mansteinstrasse 4 ☎ 2162973 🕐 Mon, Tue, Thu, Fri 4PM–midnight; Wed, Sat, Sun 11AM–1AM Ⓤ U- or S-Bahn Yorckstrasse

METROPOL

Brash and touristy, the Metropol was built in

SPORTS

BLUB

Berlin's most famous swimming pool, with indoor and outdoor facilities, boasts Europe's longest (120m) 'superslide'. Sauna and children's play area.

✚ Off map to south ✉ Buschkrugallee 64 ☎ 6066060 🍽 Restaurant and café 🚇 U-Bahn Grenzallee

BOWLING-HOUSE AM TIERPARK

Ten-pin bowling lanes, plus darts and billiards.

✚ Off map to east ✉ Otto Schmirgalstrasse 1 ☎ 5126662 🚇 U-Bahn Tierpark

FEZ (FREIZEIT-UND-ERHOLUNGSZENTRUM WUHLHEIDE)

This leisure centre in pleasant Köpenick includes a swimming pool.

✚ Off map to southeast ✉ An der Wuhlheide ☎ 530710 🍽 Café 🚇 S-Bahn Wuhlheide

OLYMPIASTADION

The stadium was built to host the 1936 Olympics. Soccer games take place here, and the swimming pool is open to the public.

✚ Off map to west ✉ Olympische Platz ☎ 3040676 🍽 Café 🚇 U-Bahn Olympiastadion (Ost)

SEEBAD FRIEDRICHSHAGEN

A beach on the eastern side of the city offering a less crowded alternative to Wannsee in the west.

✚ Off map to southeast ✉ Müggelseedamm 216 ☎ 6569731 🍽 Café 🚇 S-Bahn Friedrichshagen

SEZ (SPORT UND ERHOLUNGS-ZENTRUM)

The SEZ has a fitness studio, swimming pool, bowling alley, skating rinks, volleyball courts.

✚ N4 ✉ Landsberger Allee 77 ☎ 421820 🍽 Café 🚇 S-Bahn Landsberger Allee

SPORTPARK KARLSHORST

This enormous multi-fitness centre has all the usual training equipment plus squash, tennis and badminton courts, saunas, solarium and restaurant.

✚ Off map to southeast ✉ Rheinpfalzallee ☎ 5099391 🍽 Restaurant 🚇 S-Bahn Karlshorst

STRANDBAD WANNSEE

Wannsee's open-air pool and facilities date from the 1930s but have worn well. Near large beach.

✚ Off map to southwest ✉ Wannseebadweg ☎ 8035450 🍽 Café 🚇 S-Bahn Wannsee

TENNIS AND SQUASH CITY

The Wilmersdorf complex has 18 squash and tennis courts. Rent by the hour.

✚ Off map to south ✉ Brandenburgische Strasse 53 ☎ 8739097 🚇 U-Bahn Adenauerplatz

TRABRENNBAHN MARIENDORF

Trotting races usually take place on Sundays at this suburban racetrack.

✚ Off map to south ✉ Mariendorfer Damm 222 – 98 ☎ 8531309 🚇 U-Bahn Alt Mariendorf

Cycling

Cycling is increasingly popular with Berliners. But beware – bicyclists pay scant regard to pedestrians. Bike lights at night seem to be a luxury that many can do without. So, if you hear the frantic ringing of a bell – watch out.

LUXURY HOTELS

Prices

Expect to pay over DM300 per night for a double room at a luxury hotel.

Bristol Hotel Kempinski

Almost all of Berlin's traditional hotels were destroyed during World War II though some names, at least, live on. The Bristol Hotel Kempinski trades on a long-established reputation for courteous and attentive service. Once located on a prime site on Unter den Linden, the Bristol has now moved west to the Ku'damm, but is quieter than its location might suggest. Sadly the building is undistinguished but chandeliers and deep-piled carpets offer faint echoes of a resplendent past.

ADFON HOTEL

This historic hotel, right by the Brandenburg Gate, is one of the most luxurious in the city.

✚ H5 ✉ Pariser Platz ☎ 22610 Ⓜ S-Bahn Unter den Linden

ALSTERHOF

This small 1960s hotel near the Europa-Center has 144 rooms, a swimming pool and a fitness centre.

✚ C7 ✉ Augsburger Strasse 5 ☎ 212420 Ⓜ U-Bahn Augsburger Strasse

BERLIN EXCELSIOR HOTEL

Conveniently located near Zoo Station, the hotel boasts a garden terrace and duplex suites. There are 315 rooms and several bars, restaurants, etc.

✚ E6 ✉ Hardenbergstrasse 14 ☎ 31993 Ⓜ U- or S-Bahn Zoologischer Garten

BERLIN HILTON

Offering fabulous views over the Gendarmenmarkt, the Hilton has 320 rooms, plus restaurants, bars, a business centre and a swimming pool.

✚ J6 ✉ Mohrenstrasse 30 ☎ 20230 Ⓜ U-Bahn Stadtmitte

BRISTOL HOTEL KEMPINSKI

The Bristol has a reputation and a famous name to live up to. It has 315 rooms and 44 suites, plus a swimming pool, a fitness room and shops. (See panel.)

✚ B7 ✉ Ku'damm 27 ☎ 884340 Ⓜ U-Bahn Adenauerplatz

INTER-CONTINENTAL BERLIN

Berlin's most glamorous hotel has 511 rooms, 70 suites, a swimming pool and a sauna, shops and a business centre.

✚ F6 ✉ Budapester Strasse 2 ☎ 26020 Ⓜ U- or S-Bahn Zoologischer Garten

RADISSON PLAZA

A Swedish-designed hotel with views of the Berliner Dom, 322 rooms and VIP suites, restaurants and bars.

✚ K5 ✉ Karl-Liebknecht-Strasse 5 ☎ 23828 Ⓜ U- or S-Bahn Alexanderplatz

RESIDENZ BERLIN

Jugendstil architecture is one of the boasts of this hotel, conveniently situated for the Ku'damm. The restaurant is especially recommended.

✚ E7 ✉ Meinekestrasse 9 ☎ 884430 Ⓜ U-Bahn Kurfürstendamm

SAVOY HOTEL

An elegant hotel with large roof terrace just a minute or two's walk from the Ku'damm.

✚ E7 ✉ Fasanenstrasse 9–10 ☎ 311030 Ⓜ U-Bahn Uhlandstrasse

THE WESTIN GRAND

A five-storey ultra-modern hotel in renovated Friedrichstrasse with swimming pool and sauna.

✚ J5 ✉ Friedrichstrasse 158–164 ☎ 20270 Ⓜ U- or S-Bahn Friedrichstrasse

Mid-Range Hotels

BERLIN PLAZA HOTEL
This renovated hotel near the Ku'damm has 131 rooms and a restaurant with a terrace.
✠ D7 ✉ Knesebeckstrasse 63 ☎ 88413444 🚇 U-Bahn Uhlandstrasse

FJORD HOTEL
Clean and modern, with 65 rooms, convenient for the Kulturforum. Roof terrace open for breakfast in summer.
✠ G7 ✉ Bissingzeile 13 ☎ 254720 🚇 U-Bahn Kurfürstenstrasse

HOTEL ASTORIA
Situated among the art galleries of Fasanenstrasse. Facilities include a bar and a baby-sitting service.
✠ E6 ✉ Fasanenstrasse 2 ☎ 3124067 🚇 U-Bahn Uhlandstrasse

HOTEL BRANDENBURGER HOF
A stylish building dating back to the Wilhelmine era, not far from the Kaiser Wilhelm Memorial Church, and with a winter garden and restaurant.
✠ E7 ✉ Eislebener Strasse 14 ☎ 214050 🚇 U-Bahn Augsburger Strasse

HOTEL JURINE
Friendly family-run hotel with 53 rooms all with pay and satellite TV. Ideal location for umpires of the Prenzlauer Berg restaurant scene.
✠ K3 ✉ Schmedter Strasse 15 ☎ 443299 🚇 U-Bahn Senefelderplatz

HOTEL KRONPRINZ BERLIN
An elegant 53-room hotel, at the end of the Ku'damm.
✠ B7 ✉ Kronprinzendamm 1 ☎ 896030 🚇 S-Bahn Halensee

HOTEL MEINEKE
A rambling building, rather noisy but quite central, with 60 rooms.
✠ E7 ✉ Meinekestrasse 10 ☎ 882811 🚇 U-Bahn Uhlandstrasse

HOTEL UNTER DEN LINDEN
A modern hotel in a prime location on the corner of Unter den Linden and Friedrichstrasse, with 320 rooms and suites, restaurant, bar and conference facilities.
✠ J5 ✉ Unter den Linden 14 ☎ 238110 🚇 U- or S-Bahn Friedrichstrasse

HOTEL VILLA KASTANIA
Comfortable hotel in Charlottenburg. Rooms have good facilities, and there is a swimming pool.
✠ A6 ✉ Kastanienallee 20 ☎ 30000210 🚇 U-Bahn Theodor-Heuss-Platz

KANTHOTEL
A good location at the price, within easy reach of both the Ku'damm and the Wilmersdorfer Strasse shopping area. A modern hotel with 55 rooms.
✠ C6 ✉ Kantstrasse 111 ☎ 323026 🚇 U-Bahn Wilmersdorfer Strasse

Prices
Expect to pay up to DM300 per night for a double room in a mid-range hotel.

Hotel locations
You can stay virtually anywhere in Berlin, but hotels tend to cluster around the Ku'damm. Charlottenburg and Schöneberg are quieter but equally convenient. The establishments spawned by the East German authorities, like the Forum on Alexanderplatz or the Radisson Plaza (➤ 84), are trying desperately to cope with the chill winds of economic competition. The most scenic locations are Tegel, Wannsee, the Grunewald forest and Müggelsee.

BUDGET ACCOMMODATION

Prices

Expect to pay up to DM 150 for a double room in budget hotels.

Where to look

Berlin offers a surprising variety of lower-priced accommodation and you do not necessarily need to trek out to the backwoods. Schöneberg and Kreuzberg are both districts with a plentiful supply of pensions and one-star hotels, most of which are clean and up to scratch. Young people may prefer Kreuzberg, which has a lively night scene.

AM KROSSINSEE

Campsite open from April to October.

➕ Off map to southeast ✉ Wernsdorfer Strasse 4 ☎ 6758687 🚈 S-Bahn Köpenick

BACKPACKER

Mini-hotel with 20 beds from 27DM per night, catering specifically for backpackers. Information service; bike hire.

➕ H3 ✉ Chausseestrasse 102 ☎ 2515202 🚇 U-Bahn Zinnowitzerstrasse

CIRCUS

Downtown hostel, tailormade for backpackers with 24-hour reception, ticket service, bike hire, luggage store and no curfew.

➕ J4 ✉ Am Zirkus 2–3 ☎ 28391433 🚇 U- or S-Bahn Friedrichstrasse

DIE FABRIK

Clean, friendly hostel in an old brick factory building, ideal if you're exploring the Kreuzberg scene.

➕ M7 ✉ Schlesische Strasse 18 ☎ 6117116 🚇 U-Bahn Schlesisches Tor

FRAUEN HOTEL ARTEMISIA

A hotel just for women – and a real bargain, with attractively furnished rooms, a bar and even a library. Book early – there are only eight rooms. In Wilmersdorf.

➕ C7 ✉ Brandenburgische Strasse 18 ☎ 8738905 🚇 U-Bahn Adenauerplatz

HOTEL TRANSIT

One of the best hotels in the lower price range. The accommodation is clean, and the facilities are surprisingly good.

➕ J8 ✉ Hagelberger Strasse 53–4 ☎ 7855051 🚇 U-Bahn Mehringdamm

JUGENDGÄSTEHAUS AM WANNSEE

A clean friendly youth hostel in the scenic Grunewald.

➕ Off map to west ✉ Badeweg 1 ☎ 2623024 🚍 Bus 119, 181

JUGENDGÄSTEHAUS BERLIN

Advance booking is essential for this popular youth hostel.

➕ G6 ✉ Kluckstrasse 3 ☎ 2611097 🚇 U-Bahn Kurfürstenstrasse

MITWOHNZENTRALE

Useful for longer stays in the city, Mitwohnzentrale will arrange apartment sharing for you. A moderate fee is payable, based on the cost of the room or apartment.

CasaNostra ☎ 2355120
Domicil ☎ 7862003
Freiraum ☎ 6182008
Last Minute ☎ 7865284

PENSION KREUZBERG

A favourite with youngsters and backpackers. The location is ideal for sampling the Kreuzberg *Szene*.

➕ J7 ✉ Grossebeerenstrasse 64 ☎ 2511362 🚇 U-Bahn Mehringdamm

BERLIN
travel facts

Arriving & Departing   88

Essential Facts   88–90

Public Transport   90–91

Media &
     Communications   91-92

Emergencies   92–93

Language   93

ARRIVING & DEPARTING

Before you go

- EU nationals and citizens of the US, Canada, Australia and New Zealand require a valid passport or national identity card; all other nationals need a visa.
- No vaccination is compulsory, but have up-to-date tetanus and polio immunisation.

When to go

- Expect some rain at any time, with some unusually hot and humid weather in summer.
- April to June is the most comfortable period.

Climate

- Average temperatures: January -1°C (29°F); April 10°C (50°F); July 20°C (68°F); October 10°C (50°F).

Arriving by air

- Berlin has three international airports (Tegel, Schönefeld and Tempelhof).
- Most flights arrive at Tegel, to the north, and Schönefeld, in the east, which is being expanded. Tempelhof, in the south, handles domestic and charter flights.
- All major carriers fly to Berlin.
- Tegel (Flughafen Berlin-Tegel) 🚌 B1 ☎ 41011 for information (5AM–11:30PM) 🚍 109 to Ku'damm and Zoo Station (Bahnhof Zoo)
- Tempelhof (Flughafen Berlin-Tempelhof) 🚌 J9 ☎ 69510 🚇 U-Bahn line 6 (Platz der Luftbrücke *not* Tempelhof). Change at Friedrichstrasse for the West End 🚍 119 for Ku'damm
- Schönefeld (Flughafen Berlin-Schönefeld) 🚌 Off map to southeast ☎ 60910 🚇 S-Bahn lines 9 and 10 to Zoo station via Alexanderplatz

Arriving by bus

- Central bus station, Funkturm, Messedamm (terminus for all long-distance coaches). Travel information ☎ 3018028

Arriving by train

- Berlin has good connections from Paris, Brussels, Copenhagen, Warsaw, Moscow, Vienna and Prague.
- The main stations are Hauptbahnhof, Berlin-Lichtenberg and Zoo station (Bahnhof Zoo).
- Train information: German National Railway (Bundesbahn) 🚌 E6 ✉ Hardenbergstrasse 20 ☎ 19419. For train information ☎ 27800 (Mon–Fri 8:30–6:30)

Travelling by car

- A ring road provides access from north and south.
- Telephone a Mitfahrzentrale (ride-centre) to arrange a lift to other German cities in a private car (agree rates beforehand). Mitfahrzentralen are located at : Liebland, U-Bahn Zoo, platform 2 🚌 E6 ☎ 19440 (daily 9AM–8PM) U-Bahn Alexanderplatz 🚌 K5 ☎ 2415820 (Mon–Fri 9AM–8PM; Sat 10–6; Sun 11–4) U- or S-Bahn Yorckstrasse 🚌 H8 ☎ 19420 (Mon–Fri 9AM–8PM; Sat–Sun 10–6)

Customs regulations

- No currency restrictions.
- EU nationals need only declare items not intended for their personal use.
- Customs restrictions remain for non-EU visitors. Limits are: 200 cigarettes or 50 cigars or 250g of tobacco; 1 litre of spirits, or fortified wine – 2 litres or table wine – 3 litres; 60cc of perfume.

ESSENTIAL FACTS

Electricity

- 220 volts on a two-pin plug.

Etiquette
- It is polite to say *Guten Tag* (good day) and *Auf Wiedersehen* (goodbye) when shopping and *Entschuldigen Sie* (excuse me) in crowds.
- Never jaywalk or jump lights at pedestrian crossings.
- Informal dress is the norm when dining out in Berlin, but the usual dress rules apply in nightclubs.

Money matters
- The German unit of currency is the *Deutsche Mark* (DM 1 = 100 pfennig).
- Exchange offices (*Wechselstuben*) can be found all over Berlin: Zoo station (Bahnhof Zoo) 🚼 E6 🕐 Mon–Sat 7:30AM–10PM; Sun and holidays 8–7
Friedrichstrasse station 🚼 J5 🕐 Mon–Fri 7AM–7:30PM; Sat–Sun 8–4; holidays 9–2
Hauptbahnhof 🚼 M6 🕐 Mon–Fri 7AM–10PM; Sat 7–6; Sun 8–4
- Automatic cash dispensers (ATMs) can be found at: Sparkasse: ✉ Kantstrasse 165, Alexanderplatz 2
Commerzbank: Europa Center, ✉ Potsdamerstrasse 125; Friedrichstrasse 130; Kurfürstendamm 59
Deutsche Bank: ✉ Kurfürstendamm 28 and 182; Hardenbergstrasse 27, Alexanderplatz 6
- Most major credit cards (American Express, MasterCard, Visa, EuroCard and Diners Club) are acceptable.
- American Express Office 🚼 E7 ✉ Uhlandstrasse 173–4 ☎ 2017400
- DM traveller's cheques are preferred, but those in US Dollars and major European currencies are acceptable.

National holidays
- 1 January, Good Friday, Easter Monday, 1 May, Ascension Day, Whit Monday, 3 October (German Unity Day), November (Day of Repentance and Prayer; movable), Christmas Day, 26 December.

Opening hours
- Shops 🕐 Mon–Fri 9:30–6:30; Sat 9–2. On Thursdays some stores stay open till 8PM
- Banks 🕐 Mon–Fri 9–12:30. Afternoons vary
- Pharmacies 🕐 Mon–Fri 9:30–6:30; Sat 9–2. Late opening: Europa-Apotheke 🚼 E6 ✉ Tauentzienstrasse 9 ☎ 2614142 🕐 Daily 9AM-9PM; otherwise ☎ 01189 for pharmacy opening times

Places of worship
- Religious services information: ☎ 01157
- Protestant: Kaiser Wilhelm Memorial Church (► 34) ☎ 2185023; Services 🕐 Sun 10AM, 6PM (9AM in English during the summer)
- Berliner Dom (► 45) ☎ 20269111; Services 🕐 Sun 10AM, 6PM (Evensong in English Thu 6PM)
- Roman Catholic: Hedwigskirche (► 43) ☎ 2034810; Masses 🕐 Sun 8AM, 10AM, 11:30AM, 6PM; Sat 7PM
- Anglican: St George's 🚼 Off map to west ✉ Preussenallee; Holy Communion 🕐 Sun 8AM; Morning service 🕐 Sun 10AM
- Jewish: Conservative Synagogue 🚼 D6 ✉ Pestalozzistrasse 14 ☎ 3138411; Services 🕐 Fri 6PM; Sat 9:30AM; Orthodox Synagogue 🚼 J4 ✉ Adass Jisroel, Tucholsky Strasse 40; Services 🕐 Fri 5PM; Sat 9:30AM

Student travellers
- Discounts of up to 50 per cent in museums and some theatres are available with an International Student Identity Card.
- The Bundesbahn offers special rail fares for young people holding a *Reisepasse*.
- European 'Transalpino' tickets are also available for people under 26.
- For youth hostels ► 86.

Time differences
- Berlin is one hour ahead of Greenwich Mean Time in winter and two hours ahead in summer.

Tipping
- A service charge is usually included in hotel and restaurant bills. It is usual to tip porters, washroom attendants and maids.

Toilets
- Men = *Herren*; Women = *Damen* or *Frauen*.
- Public toilets are free but scarce. Use those in cafés, restaurants, hotels and department stores.

Women travellers
- Schokofabrik (Women's Center):
  ⊞ L7 ✉ Marianenstrasse 6
  ☎ 6152440 ⊕ Café: Mon–Fri 1PM–midnight; Sun noon–2PM. Turkish bath: Sun–Fri 11–10
- Women's Hotel: Artemisia (► 86)

PUBLIC TRANSPORT

- Berlin has an excellent public transport network, with two urban railways and numerous bus and tram routes. The local transport authority is the Berliner Verkehrs-Betriebe (BVG).
- Information: BVG-Pavillon ⊞ E6
  ✉ Hardenbergplatz (Zoo station) ☎ 29712971 travel information ☎ 19419 customer services
  ⊕ Mon–Fri 8–6; Sat 7–2; Sun 9–4
- BVG lost property: BVG Tempelhof ⊞ Off map to south
  ✉ Lorenzweg 5 ☎ 25623040

Types of ticket
- The **24-hour ticket** (Berlin-Ticket or *24-Stunden-Karte*) and the weekly or monthly *Umweltkarte* allow unlimited travel on the entire BVG network (trains, buses, trams and the ferry from Wannsee to Kladow).

Umweltkarten are transferable to other users. The weekly ticket is valid Mon–Sat; a separate day ticket is required for Sunday.
- A **single ticket** is valid for two hours. You can transfer or interrupt your journey.
- The *Kurzstreckentarif* (short-distance ticket) is valid on the U- and S-Bahn for up to three stops including transfers, or for one line only on buses and trams.
- The *Sammelkarte* (multiple ticket) must be stamped before each journey in the red ticket machines in buses and at station entrances.
- **BerlinWelcomeCard** entitles one adult and up to three children to free BVG travel for three days as well as reductions on sightseeing trips, museums, theatres and other attractions. Enquire at your hotel, tourist information offices or U-Bahn ticket offices.

Discounts
- Children under 14 travel at reduced rates; children under six are free.

The metro
- Berlin's two networks, known as U-Bahn (underground railway) and S-Bahn (city railway), are complementary and interchangeable.
- First buy a ticket from station foyers or from vending machines on platforms. Routes are referred to by the final stop on the line.
- You must validate your ticket at a machine on the platform before boarding the train.
- Trains run every five or ten minutes, Mon–Fri 4AM–1AM; Sat–Sun 4AM–2AM (approximately). On Friday and Saturday nights, trains on U-Bahn lines 1 and 9 run throughout the night at 15-minute intervals.

- You may take bicycles on the U-Bahn on weekdays 9AM–2PM, after 5:30PM, and all weekend. Cyclists may travel on the S-Bahn at any time. There is a small charge. (Holders of Umweltkarten and Berlin-Ticket travel free.)

Buses
- Central Bus Station, Funkturm ☎ 3018028
- Enter the cream-coloured double-deckers at the front and leave by the doors in the middle or at the back. Pay the driver with small change or show ticket (see above). Multiple tickets, also valid for U- and S-Bahn, can be bought from vending machines at some bus stops or at U-Bahn stations, but not from the driver.
- Route 100 is particularly useful, departing from Zoo station and linking the West End with Unter den Linden and Alexanderplatz.
- More than 40 night buses operate half-hourly from 1AM to 4AM. Line N19 runs through the centre every 15 minutes.
- Buses have rear-door access and safety straps for wheelchairs.
- Wheelchair users may find the Telebus service useful: Telebus-Zentrale ✚ E7 ✉ Joachimstaler Strasse 17 ☎ 4775440

Trams
- Trams operate largely in eastern Berlin. Ticket procedures are the same as for buses.

Maps and timetables
- Obtain timetables and maps from the BVG-Pavillon (➤ 90) and from U-Bahn station ticket offices. Tourist Information Offices also have transport information.

Taxis
- Taxis are good value, with stands throughout the city. Only use cabs with a meter.
- There is a small surcharge for baggage.
- Not all drivers know their way around, so have a map with you!
- Contact numbers ☎ 69022, 261026, 210101, 210202, 691001
- Chauffeur service ☎ 2139090

BVG ferries
- BVG ferry lines in the Wannsee and Köpenick areas include services from Wannsee to Kladow, Glienicker Bridge to Sacrow, Grünau to Wendenschloss and around Müggelsee.

MEDIA & COMMUNICATIONS

Telephones
- Phone boxes marked *Kartentelefon* use phone cards (from post offices).
- Boxes marked *International* and telephones in post offices are for long-distance calls.
- Calls are cheapest after 10PM and on Sundays.
- Follow the dialling instructions in several languages in the box.
- For local enquiries dial 01188.
- International enquiries 00118.
- The code for Germany is 0049.
- The code for Berlin from abroad is 030.
- To call the UK dial 0044.
- For the US dial 001.
- Operator (local) 03; (international) 0010.

Post offices
- Normal opening hours 🕐 Mon–Fri 8–6; Sat 8–noon. Some stay open to 8:30PM Thu
- Poste Restante (*Hauptpostlagernd*): use the post office at Zoo station 🕐 Mon–Sat 6AM-midnight; Sun 8AM–midnight ☎ 3110020
- US citizens can receive mail at the

American Express Office
✉ Ku'damm 11 ☎ 8827575

- Other main post offices ✉ Marburger Strasse 12–13; ✉ Goethestrasse 2–3; ✉ Hauptbahnhof
- Stamps can be bought from vending machines on the Ku'damm as well as post offices.
- Postboxes are bright yellow.

Newspapers

- National dailies published in Berlin include *Die Welt* and *Bild*.
- Local dailies include *Tagesspiegel*, *Tageszeitung*, *Berliner Morgenpost*, *Berliner Zeitung*, *Berliner Kurier*.
- Most large hotels and newsstands stock the major European dailies and *International Herald Tribune*.
- Useful listings magazines include: *Tip*, *Zitty* (both twice monthly, German); *Berlin TutGut* (from Tourist Information, in English); *Berlin Das Magazin* (quarterly, in English/German); *Berlin Programm* (monthly, in German).

Radio

- BBC World Service is available locally on 90.2FM.

Television

- Major hotels provide CNN and BBC news broadcasts, an English-language sports channel and the music channel MTV.
- *Zitty* magazine lists programmes.

EMERGENCIES

Sensible precautions

- Berlin is one of the safer European cities, but you should always remain on your guard.
- Avoid poorly lit areas, especially around Potsdamer Platz.
- Potsdamer Strasse is the centre of a seedy red-light district.
- Thieves often target tourists on the U-Bahn, so keep wallets and purses concealed.
- Bicycle theft is common, so if you hire a bike keep it locked.

Lost property

- Police, Tempelhof ✚ J9 ✉ Platz der Luftbrücke 6 ☎ 6990
- Central Lost and Found ☎ 6995
- BVG Transport Lost and Found ☎ 25623040

Medical and dental treatment

- Travel insurance is advisable. EU nationals are entitled to free medical treatment on production of the form E111, obtainable from post offices in your native country.
- There are plenty of English-speaking doctors in Berlin.
- Emergency services:
  Medical ☎ 310031
  Dental ☎ 8900433
  Poison ☎ 19240

Medicines

- Remember to take any specially prescribed medications with you.
- For pharmacy opening hours ➤ 89.

Emergency phone numbers

- Coins are not needed for emergency calls from public telephones:
  Police ☎ 110
  Fire ☎ 112
  Ambulance ☎ 115
- Travelers' Aid (in Zoo Station) ☎ 3138088
- American Hotline: crisis hotline ☎ 0177 8141510

Embassies and Consulates in Berlin

- USA ✉ Neustädtischer Kirchstrasse 4–5 ☎ 8329233
- UK ✉ Unter den Linden 32–4 ☎ 201840
- Australia ✉ Kempinski Plaza, Uhlandstrasse 181–3 ☎ 8800880
- Canada ✉ IHZ Building, Friedrichstrasse 95

☎ 2611161
- Ireland ✉ Ernst-Reuter-Platz 10
  ☎ 34800822

German National Tourist Organisation offices overseas

- UK ✉ 65 Curzon Street, London W1Y 7PE
  ☎ 0171-317 0908 (Mon–Fri 10–12 and 2–4) or
  0891-600 100 (recorded message)
- USA ✉ 747 Third Avenue, 33rd Floor, New
  York, NY 10017 ☎ (212) 661 7200
- Australia ✉ Lufthansa House, 12th Floor, 143
  Macquerie Street, Sydney 2000 ☎ (02) 926 78148

Tourist information offices

- Verkehrsamt Berlin, Europa-
  Center ✚ E6 ✉ Budapester Strasse
  ☎ 2626031 🕐 Mon–Sat 8AM–10PM; Sun 9–9
- Airport Tegel ☎ 41013145
  🕐 Daily 8AM–11PM
- Hauptbahnhof ☎ 2795209
  🕐 Daily 8–8
- Bahnhof Zoo (Zoo station)
  ☎ 3139063/4 🕐 Mon–Sat 8AM–11PM
- Brandenburger Tur
  🕐 Daily 9:30AM–6PM
- Berlin Tourismus Marketing
  GmbH ✉ Am Karlsbad 11 ☎ 230025

LANGUAGE

yes	ja	dinner	das Abendessen
no	nein	white wine	der Weisswein
please	bitte	red wine	der Rotwein
thank you	danke	beer	das Bier
good morning	guten Morgen	bread	das Brot
good evening	guten Abend	milk	die Milch
good night	gute Nacht	sugar	der Zucker
goodbye	auf Wiedersehen	water	das Wasser
today	heute	bill	die Rechnung
yesterday	gestern	room	das Zimmer
tomorrow	morgen	on the right	rechts
small	klein	on the left	links
large	gross	straight on	geradeaus
quickly	schnell	open	offen
good	gut	closed	geschlossen
menu	die Speisekarte	how much?	wieviel?
breakfast	das Frühstück	expensive	teuer
lunch	das Mittagessen	cheap	billig

excuse me please
　　　　　　entschuldigen Sie bitte
do you speak English?
　　　　　　sprechen SieEnglisch?
I don't speak German
　　　　Ich spreche kein Deutsch
I don't understand Ich verstehe nicht

train station	der Bahnhof
airport	der Flughafen
luggage	das Gepäck
bank	die Bank
post office	das Postamt
police	die Polizei
hospital	das Krankenhaus
doctor	der Arzt
Monday	Montag
Tuesday	Dienstag
Wednesday	Mittwoch
Thursday	Donnerstag
Friday	Freitag
Saturday	Samstag /Sonnabend
Sunday	Sonntag

one	eins	eleven	elf
two	zwei	twelve	zwölf
three	drei	thirteen	dreizehn
four	vier	fourteen	vierzehn
five	fünf	fifteen	fünfzehn
six	sechs	twenty	zwanzig
seven	sieben	twenty-one	
eight	acht		ein-und-zwanzig
nine	neun	fifty	fünfzig
ten	zehn	hundred	hundert

93

INDEX

A

Abbado, Claudio 9
accommodation 84–6
airports 88
Alexanderplatz 47
Allied Forces
    Museum 50
Applied Art, Museum of
    36, 48

B

Babelsberg Film Studio
    15, 59
Bauhaus Museum 34
Bell Tower of Olympic
    Stadium 57
Berlin Cathedral 45
Berlin Museum 50
Berlin Wall 12, 40
Berlin Working-class
    Life, Museum of 51
Berliner Schloss 45
Berliners 6–7
Bernau 20
Blockhaus
    Nikolskoe 63
boat tours 19
Bode Museum 43
Botanical Garden 56
Brandenburg 21
Brandenburg Gate 39
Brecht's House 50
Breitscheidplatz 33
Britzer Garten 56
Bröhan Museum 50
Brücke Museum 52
buses and trams 88, 91

C

cabaret 79
cash dispensers 89
Cecilienhof, Schloss 25
Charlottenburg,
    Schloss 31
Checkpoint Charlie 40
City Hall 47
city tours 19
climate 88
credit cards 89
crime 92
currency 89
customs regulations 88
cycling 60, 83, 92

D

Deutsche Staatsoper
    42, 78
Deutscher Dom 41
Diepgen, Eberhard 9
driving 88

E

Eastside Gallery 52
economy 8
Egyptian Museum 50
electricity 88
Elisabethkirche 16
embassies and
    consulates 92–3
emergencies 92–3
Ephraimpalais 46
Ethnographical
    Museum 30
etiquette 89
Europa-Center 77
events 22, 82
excursions 19, 20–1

F

Federal government 7
Fernsehturm 47
ferry services 91
Fischer-Dieskau,
    Dietrich 9
folk, jazz and rock 82
food and drink
    bars 80-1
    cafés 32, 68–9
    eating out 62–9
    food shops 75
Französischer Dom 41
Frederick the Great
    12, 42
Freizeitpark Tegel 56
Friedrichs-Brücke 54
Friedrichwerdersche
    Kirche 53
Funkturm 57

G

galleries, commercial 73
Gemäldegalerie 35
Gendarmenmarkt 41
German History
    Museum 42
German Resistance,
    Memorial to 55
Gertraudenbrücke 54
Gethsemane Kirche 53
Glienicker Brücke 26
Globe Fountain 33
'Gold Else' 37
Gothic House 27
Grips-Theater 59
Grunewald 28
Grunewaldsee 28
Grunewaldturm 28

H

Hedwigkirche 42
history 10-11
Hitler, Adolf 12, 17, 55
hotels 84–6
Huguenot Museum 41
Humboldt University 42
hunting museum 28

I

Iduna House 32
immunisation 88
Indian & East Asian Art,
    Museums of 51
itineraries 14-15

J

Jagdschloss Grunewald 28
Jungfernbrücke 54

K

Kaiser Wilhelm
    Memorial
    Church 33
Käthe Kollwitz
    memorial 16
Käthe Kollwitz
    Museum 32
Klein-Glienicke,
    Schloss 26
Kleistpark 17
Kleist's Grave 58
Klosterhof 26
Knoblauchhaus 46
Königliche Porzellan
    Manufaktor
    (KPM) 74
Konzerthaus 41
Köpenick, Schloss 48
Kreuzberg 7, 18
Krumme Lanke 28
Kulturforum 35
Kupferstich-Kabinett 52
Kurfürstendamm 32

L

Langes Luch 28
language (basic
    vocabulary) 93
Lessingbrücke 54
Literaturhaus 32
lost property 92
Lübbenau 20–1
Lustgarten 45
Lutherhaus 20

Lutherstadt
    Wittenberg 20
Luxemburg, Rosa 37, 54

M

Marienkirche 47
markets 75
Marmorpalais 25
Marx and Engels
    (sculptures) 58
Matschinsky-Denninghof
    sculpture 58
Matthäikirche 35
medical treatment 92
medicines 92
metro 90–1
'The Missing House' 16
Moabiter Brücke 54
Moltkebrücke 54
Monbijou Park 59
money 89
'Mont Klamott' 57
Moore, Henry
    (sculpture) 58
Müggelturm 57
Museums Island 43
Musical Instruments,
    Museum of 35

N

Napoleon 12
national holidays 89
Neue Wache 42
New National Gallery 35
New Palace 24
New Synagogue 51, 53
newspapers 92
nightclubs 80–1
Nikolaikirche 46
Nikolaiviertel 46

O

Oberbaumbrücke 54
Old Royal Library 42
opening hours 89

P

Pariser Platz 39
Park Babelsberg 57
passports and visas 88
Peacock Island 59
Pergamon Museum 44
personal safety 92
pharmacies 89
places of worship 89
Plötzensee Memorial 55
population 8
post offices 91–2

Potsdam Conference 25
Potsdam Film Museum
    15, 51
Potsdamer Platz 6
Pre- and Early History,
    Museum of 32
Prenzlauer Berg 16
Prinz-Albrecht-Palais 39
public transport 90–1

Q

Quadriga 39

R

radio and television 92
rail services 88, 90–1
Rathaus Schöneberg
    17, 55
Regierungsviertel 7, 38
Reichstag 55

S

Sachsenhausen 29
Sanssouci, Schloss 24
Savignyplatz 18
Scheunenviertel 16
Schinkel, KF, 26, 31, 39,
    41, 42, 53, 54, 56
Schleusenbrücke 54
Schlossbrücke 54
Schlossinsel 48
Schöneberg 17
seasons 88
shopping 70–7, 89
Siegessäule 37
Sophienkirche 53
Soviet War Memorial 58
Spandau 27
sport 83
Spreewald 20
student travellers 89–90

T

taxis 91
telephone numbers,
    emergency 92
telephones 91
Teufelsberg 28
theatres and concerts 78
Tiergarten 6, 37
Tierpark Berlin-
    Friedrichsfelde 56
time differences 90
toilets 90
Topography of Terror 38
tourist offices 93
Transport & Technology
    Museum 51, 59

traveller's cheques 89
travelling to Berlin 88
Treptower Park 56

U

Unter den Linden 42

V

Viktoriapark 56
Villa Grisebach 32
Volkspark
    Jungfernheide 56

W

walks 16–18, 19
Wannsee Centre 55
Wannsee-Kladow ferry 60
Wars of Liberation,
    Monument to the 56
Wilhelm II, Kaiser 12, 25,
    28, 33
Winterfeldtplatz 17, 75
Wittenbergplatz
    U-Bahn 60
women travellers 90

Z

Zeiss-Grossplanetarium
    59
Zeughaus 42
Zille 58
Zitadelle 27
Zoo and Aquarium 59
Zum Nussbaum 46

CityPack
Berlin

Written by   Christopher and Melanie Rice

Edited, designed and produced by
  AA Publishing

Maps   © The Automobile Association 1996, 1999
Fold-out map © RV Reise- und Verkehrsverlag Munich · Stuttgart
  © Cartography: GeoData

Distributed in the United Kingdom by AA Publishing, Norfolk House, Priestley Road, Basingstoke, Hampshire, RG24 9NY.

© The Automobile Association 1996, 1999
First published 1996
Revised second edition 1999

ISBN 0 7495 1956 8

Published by AA Publishing (a trading name of Automobile Association Developments Limited, whose registered office is Norfolk House, Priestley Road, Basingstoke, Hampshire RG24 9NY. Registered number 1878835).

Colour separation by Daylight Colour Art Pte Ltd, Singapore
Printed and bound by Dai Nippon Printing Co (Hong Kong) Ltd.

Acknowledgements

The Automobile Association would like to thank the following photographers, libraries and associations for their assistance in the preparation of this book. Bauhaus-Archiv, Berlin (Gunteer Lepowski) 49b, Rex Features Ltd 9.
All remaining pictures are held in the Association's own library (AA PHOTO LIBRARY) and were taken by CLIVE SAWYER, with the exception of pages 17, 32, 48a, 48b, 51, 55, 57, which were taken by A BAKER; pages 1, 2, 5a, 13a, 13b, 23a, 28, 30a, 30b, 31a, 31b, 33a, 33b, 34, 36b, 37a, 37b, 39a, 41b, 43, 44, 45b, 47a, 50, 53, 56, 59, 60, 61a, 61b, 87a, which were taken by A SOUTER; and pages 49a, 87b, taken by D TRAVERSO.

The authors are grateful to the following for assistance in the updating of this book: AB Airlines, Gabriella Schiller (Berlin Philharmonic Orchestra), Natascha Kompatzki and Dr Buri (Berlin Tourismus Marketing).

REVISION VERIFIERS *Christopher and Melanie Rice*
ORIGINAL COPY-EDITOR *Julia Brittain*   INDEXER *Marie Lorimer*
SECOND EDITION UPDATED BY *OutHouse Publishing Services*

Titles in the CityPack series
● Amsterdam ● Atlanta ● Bangkok ● Barcelona ● Beijing ● Berlin ● Boston ●
● Brussels & Bruges ● Chicago ● Dublin ● Florence ● Hong Kong ● Istanbul ●
● Lisbon● London ● Los Angeles ● Madrid ● Miami ● Montréal ● Moscow
● Munich ● New York ● Paris ● Prague ● Rome ● San Francisco ● Seattle ●
● Shanghai ● Singapore ● Sydney ● Tokyo ● Toronto ● Venice ● Vienna ●
● Washington DC ●